CARVING FACES, CARVING LIVES

PEOPLE OF THE BOREAL FOREST

Text and Photographs by Terry Garvin

Heritage Community Foundation

Published by the Heritage Community Foundation
Suite 54, 9912 – 106 Street
Edmonton, Alberta, Canada
T5K 1C5

Design and graphics by Matthias Reinicke, Lime Design Inc.
Printed by Hignell Book Printing

Funding for the production and printing of *Carving Faces, Carving Lives* was provided by Alberta Aboriginal Affairs and Northern Development, Talisman Energy Inc., and West Fraser Mills Ltd.

Library and Archives Canada Cataloguing in Publication

Garvin, Terry

Carving faces, carving lives : people of the boreal forest / text and photographs by Terry Garvin.

Includes index.
ISBN 0-9739892-0-3 (bound).--ISBN 0-9739892-1-1 (pbk.)

1. Indians of North America--Canada, Northern. I.Heritage Community Foundation (Alta.) II. Title.

E78.C2G373 2005 971.9004'97'09152 C2005-907437-X

Front cover image: Katy Sanderson, Fort McMurray, 1993.

Contents

Preface

Carving Faces, Carving Lives: People of the Boreal Forest has been a labour of love for author and photographer Terry Garvin. It is at once the story of one soul's personal journey of discovery and a written and visual record of a people's changing way of life in the Northwest.

In 1951, Terry Garvin left his farm home at Craik, Saskatchewan, to enter a thirteen-year career with the Royal Canadian Mounted Police. At various times, he was stationed in northern Alberta, northern British Columbia, and the Northwest Territories, regions where a large portion of the population is made up of First Nations People. In 1964, Mr. Garvin made a career change and became a community development worker, a job that placed him in close contact with many Aboriginal residents of many northern communities. His photograph hobby, coupled with his desire to learn as much as possible about Aboriginal cultures, resulted in the acquisition of the material presented in this book.

While *Carving Faces, Carving Lives* was written primarily for students of boreal forest Aboriginal culture in Canada, it may be used by anyone who wishes to gain a better understanding of the Peoples whose heritage spans 7,000 years. The families and individuals presented in this book lived a traditional lifestyle intimately dependant on the resources of the land. Through photographs and written text, this book reveals the tremendous skill and knowledge required to sustain such a lifestyle. This is a down-to-earth, realistic documentation of that knowledge, captured by someone who felt privileged to have been there and who was given the opportunity to present the material in a way that truly honours the people in the book and the diverse cultures they represent.

Acknowledgements

I would like to thank, first and foremost, the people in this book, who were so generous. Many people validated the information contained here, but I especially want to thank Fred McDonald, Fort McKay, and Cecile Young, Bigstone Indian Band, Wabasca, who reviewed the manuscript for content. Shirley Nelson of Sherwood Park served regularly as an informal advisor. I must also thank the staff at the Aseniwuche Winewak Nation, particularly David MacPhee and Rachelle McDonald, and the Board of Directors for Aseniwuche Winewak First Nation for endorsing this publication.

Jamie Honda-McNeil was tireless in his support of the project. I am grateful to the Honourable Pearl Calahasen, Minister, Alberta Aboriginal Affairs and Northern Development, Talisman Energy Inc., and West Fraser Mills Ltd. for their funding, and to Anton Brereton and Sylvia Vance at the Heritage Community Foundation for their work on the project.

Many people encouraged me to do what I could to have the material published, in particular Rod Hyde, long-time school principal of the Fort McKay School and his wife Dorothy, previously the Chief of the Fort McKay First Nations.

I must thank my family, who endured my many reviews of the status, over several years, of this venture I was on.

The Author

In 1951, Terry Garvin, the author of this book and photographer of the images featured therein, left his farm home at Craik, Saskatchewan, to enter a thirteen-year career with the Royal Canadian Mounted Police. He was stationed in northern Alberta, northern British Columbia, and in the Northwest Territories, where a large portion of the population is made up of First Nations people. In 1964, he made a career change to be a community development worker, primarily with Aboriginal residents. This time in the north, and subsequent work in similar communities, was interrupted only by a two-year job in Indonesia and the time it took to complete a Bacbelor of Arts degree at the University of Alberta. His photograph hobby, coupled with his wish to learn as much as possible about Aboriginal cultures, resulted in the acquisition of the material represented in this book.

While *Carving Faces, Carving Lives* was written for those in the study of boreal forest Aboriginal culture in Canada, it may be used by anyone who wishes to gain a better understanding of the people whose heritage spans 7,000 years. This book reveals the tremendous skill and knowledge that sustained a traditional lifestyle intimately dependant on the resources of the land. Many of the people in this book lived that lifestyle.

It was this unwavering respect for the land and the culture sustained by it that attracted Terry to the idea of recording the knowledge and skill so many people talked to him about. This is a down-to-earth, realistic documentation of that knowledge, captured by someone who, firstly, felt privileged to have been there, and secondly, was given the opportunity to present the material in a way that truly honours the people in the book and the culture they represent.

Introduction

This book illustrates an aspect of the traditional lifestyle of the Aboriginal people of Canada's boreal forests. These forests extend as far north as the forests around Aklavik, in the Northwest Territories; from the Yukon east to Labrador; and south to the prairies. While some of the cultural practices shown are unique to the people of specific regions, these people's Aboriginal ancestry is their common bond. There are several language groups throughout the forest: the people featured in this book speak Cree, Chipewyan, Dogrib, and Dene (Slavey and Beaver).

What is common to all the people in this book is that they are hunters and gatherers whose traditional way of life was derived from the land in a forest region of northwest Canada. It is in the context of these common cultural practices that this story is told. Cultural practices vary within the range of communities in this story. The author became aware of customs which are specific to some communities and not to others. The examples which follow are briefly described.

From 1955 to 1956, while the author lived at Fort Rae, the following three customs significantly influenced the character of the Dogrib people:

(1) They believed in a creature called Negaw that roamed the mainland during the spring only. This creature was dangerous to the safety of a Dogrib person while that person was on the mainland. The Fort Rae community land base consisted of three islands, a safe place to live in the spring. Mainland activity was suspended, including government and private agency translation and guiding services. In 1967, while attending a mental health conference in Yellowknife, the author was told by Dogrib people that this custom was a major reason for some peoples' refusal to move to the government-initiated mainland community of Edzo when it was developed in the 1960s.

(2) The Dogrib people believed that the wolf was the reincarnation of their people. Although they are a trapping and hunting culture, they would not kill a wolf. It is disrespectful of visitors to wear wolf fur trim on parkas. Instead, wolverine fur, muskrat fur, beaver fur, fox fur, and hare fur were used as trim by the Dogrib people.

(3) No woman in the Dogrib community remained childless if she was physically unable to have a child of her own. She adopted a child, preferably her sister's child. The author was told that this custom was somewhat negatively influenced by the government family allowance program which effectively placed a cash value on every child.

The government of the Dogrib people was led by Chief Jimmy Bruno, who maintained power and influence by assuming responsibility for the public action of his followers. In a one-year period known to the author, there was only one "white man's" court case, a hunting violation in which legal action was initiated by the Northwest Territories Fish and Wildlife Officer. There was no police initiated court action during that period. What little need there was to handle community infractions was dealt with by local custom. The author was the police constable in charge of the region.

The Prophet River people in northern British Columbia follow the custom of Dream Mapping. Local legend, supported by traditional belief, is that a member of this First Nations community has "dreaming power", a special gift to dream and prophecy the future. The prophecy is illustrated with images drawn on a tanned moose hide, known as the map. The Prophet River Band office has a photograph of a map publicly displayed on an office wall. The author visited that community several times in 1991 and met a Dream Mapper named Fred Jumbie. Jumbie invited this author on a two-week horseback trip of his traditional lands, an offer that was accepted with pleasure but never came to fruition. The Prophet River peoples' traditional land base is 8,000 square miles (20,720 square kilometres) as evidenced by the placement of known grave sites. Their licensed trapping area is 1,600 square miles (4,144 square kilometres), while the community land they have exclusive rights to live on today is one-and-a-half square miles (almost four square kilometres).

First Nations people at Calling Lake, Alberta, practise a custom of carving a human-like facial image into a log and placing the log at the entrance of a Sweat Lodge. It was the author's privilege to be briefed in the Sweat Lodge custom over an eight-month period. The story, as recounted in this book, was told and recorded in detail at the final Sweat Lodge Ceremony. The people who granted permission to publish this account of a Sweat did so by saying that they "worry that one hundred years from now no one will know of this custom if it is not written". They speculated that the oral tradition of handing down knowledge is not as effective now as it once was.

Language influences the Aboriginal way of viewing the environment. This book was not written and produced without at least a modest awareness of language customs. The University of Alberta granted second language competency in Cree to the author in fulfilment of a Bachelor of Arts degree. A glossary of terms, the language of the bush, is included in this book to help the reader form an appreciation of the role of language. The word "tree" is an animate one in Cree, but an inanimate one in English. The author imagined that how the forest was perceived by the Aboriginal culture is somewhat different than how it is perceived by the culture of the author. Language customs, not all included in this book, influenced the author's understanding of the traditional lifestyle of people in this story.

The reader is encouraged to be aware of the cultural diversity of First Nations Peoples. Not all First Nations Peoples are alike. However, hunting, gathering, and production practices are common to all First Nations cultures, and are the focus of this publication. There are other productions which address being, knowing, substance, essence, cause, identity, time, space, and spiritual beliefs. Possibly, future publications will record more of these tremendously interesting and valuable concepts.

The people of all communities in this story are hunters, gatherers, and producers of products from land resources. Their traditional hunting, gathering, and production practices grew from dependence on the natural resources of the land, the bush, and the water. Their accounts, if not taken from their own experience, include information learned from Elders, and passed along in the stories told by their parents and grandparents. We imagine that some of the lifestyle practices still in use today were known thousands of years ago, when the distant ancestors of today's Aboriginal people settled the bushlands. Common knowledge suggests that it is only in the past three hundred years or less that the ancestors of people in this book have co-existed with other cultures.

The photographs and text illustrate the skills which have long enabled Aboriginal people to live and prosper in the traditional ways: by hunting, trapping, fishing, and the production of food and clothing and the fashioning of art, crafts, and utensils from the raw material of the forest. This information, collected between 1954 and 2000, was provided by many people, most of whom are named, and some of whom are pictured in the book. Some of the information derives from knowledge common to all bushland people, who have shared knowledge and social skill over many centuries. There is some information which is not directly credited to a name or address. The term "and many people" is used to identify an extended source of information.

The author made several dog team trips (the longest being approximately five hundred and fifty kilometres [three hundred and forty miles]) with guide and interpreter/translator Jimmy Fish, visiting Dogrib people's hunting and trapping camps situated north of Fort Rae, Northwest Territories. In January 1956, the author joined fifty-five Dogrib First Nations people in a caribou hunt that tracked a herd estimated to be 25,000 in number and required the use of dog teams totalling two hundred and fifty dogs.

This is original source data. The author's intention is to honour the people and the culture they represent, and credit them with the knowledge and skills shown in this story. This book will help students of Aboriginal cultures understand the rich cultural heritage of First Nations bushland people. All photos, with the exception of some of the art and craft items, were taken in the natural surrounding, or home base, of the subject. The author is the sole photographer of the images in this book.

Much of the data in *Carving Faces, Carving Lives* has been informally validated through the author's association since 1990 with Traditional Knowledge Studies community researchers Fred MacDonald, Cecelia Boucher, and Bertha Cantor of Fort McKay; Dwayne Desjarlais, Grant Golosky, and Elmer Cree of Fort McMurray; Cecile Young, Clayton Auger, and George Auger of Wabasca-Demerais; François Auger-Cardinal of Calling Lake; David McPhee, Rachelle McDonald, Elizabeth McDonald, and Doris McDonald of Aseniwuche Winewak First Nation of Grand Cache; Lorraine Wolf of Prophet River, and all the people named in the book.

Upon the request of the author, Fred MacDonald and Cecile Young, both with personal and family ties to the heritage this book represents, reviewed the manuscript to ensure there were no glaring errors in the author's interpretation of content. Photograph slide presentations have been made to many schools, including northern schools with a large Aboriginal student enrollment. After the manuscript was complete, a photograph slide presentation was made to an audience of Elders at Fort McKay, Hinton, and Sunchild First Nations. This material is endorsed by the people whose culture it represents.

The University of Calgary Press sponsored four reviews of the manuscript, two reviews within the University and two independent external reviews, which declared that the material was academically sound.

Fred and Cecile reviewed and edited the content of the manuscript. All of the people named in the book, and some who have not been named, validated the data by their frank and honest enthusiasm for sharing the knowledge of their culture.

Fred MacDonald, member of the Fort McKay Métis (Fort McKay).

Cecile Young, Clayton Auger, François Auger-Cardinal, and Rose Cardinal.

Cecile Young, member of the Bigstone First Nations, Athabasca.

Kyla Auger (Wabasca, 1995).

The children, grandchildren, and great grandchildren of the people whose knowledge is preserved in this book may no longer need traditional skills to survive in the bush. These children are on a lifetime adventure which may only reflect their ancient culture. Many of them, however, still want to understand their heritage whether or not they live it on a daily basis.

Genelle Richards (Conklin, 1993).

Left to right: Correne, Noreen, Simon Lemagrie Sr., and Simon Jr.

The change from a trapline to a town lifestyle can occur in a single generation. While Simon Lemagrie Sr. was raised in a trapline camp, his children live in a community with schools and other services. In his youth, Simon Sr. had few choices except the trapping and hunting lifestyle that he loves. His children will have the opportunity to pursue many vocations, and may yet choose the precarious fur industry.

Pesim and Cody Johnson of Calling Lake are among the many young people being tutored by community Elders in Aboriginal history and tradition.

Lina with a hare (rabbit) skin quilt similar to one she recalls sleeping under as a child. Lina was born at Fond Du Lac, Saskatchewan, a community on the shore of Lake Athabasca. For the first eight years of her life she knew only the language and customs of her family's trapping and hunting lifestyle. Between the ages of eight and sixteen, she lived at the Grouard Mission where she received her early schooling, an education which was unrelated to the environment of her birth place. She later married and raised a family in the urban culture of Bragg Creek and Calgary, Alberta.

Lina Gallup, nee Shott.

Hare (rabbit) fur quilt. Approximately three hundred hare pelts, cut into strips and folded to expose fur on both sides, are pieced together and woven to form a quilt.

Lina Gallup's daughter Holly and Holly's children will learn from their mother and grandmother about the traditional culture into which Lina was born. A lifestyle in a bushland Aboriginal culture, although still an option to people who succeeded their parents and grandparents, is not likely to be a lifetime choice of Lina's offspring. This extended family, as do many families, represents a dramatic lifestyle switch from the traditional trapping and hunting culture of the senior member of this family to an urban and highly industrialized culture of the younger members. The Aboriginal boreal forest cultural heritage of this family is at least 7,000 years old. Like Lina's extended family, many other extended families share the culture of change. Much of the change, from an Aboriginal bushland cultural practice to an urban industrialized culture, has happened within the lifetime of the current population of grandmothers and grandfathers. This book is their story. Their love and affection for their Aboriginal culture is reflected in the conservation and preservation of their knowledge, their arts and crafts, and things that are remarkable and worthy of remembrance (Lina's hare skin quilt, for example).

Holly Fortier and her children, Billie Sue, Jesse, and Rees (1997).

Below: Mary and Benjamin Marcel and their granddaughter Michelle. When this photograph was taken, their home was located on reserved land along the Athabasca River, near the river outlet to Lake Athabasca. They were approximately forty-eight kilometres (thirty miles) south of their shopping centre, Fort Chipewyan, the oldest continuously inhabited community in Alberta. The older couple did not participate in the huge oil sands development which was impacting their region. Michelle Marcel would grow up in a world where her life decisions would be influenced by the effects of industry (1980).

Above: Willis Flett was a child of Fort Chipewyan at a time when Aboriginal traditional lifestyle influenced the culture of his community. The community has since felt the impact of oil sands industrial development which crept its way north along the Athabasca River (1980).

Charlie Peter Nitsiza at an island in Russell Lake, waiting his turn to board the canoe that will take him, his family, and others on a four hundred kilometre (two hundred forty-nine mile) journey to the Barren Lands region to hunt caribou. During this period, families often travelled as a unit to access their hunting and trapping areas during summer and winter (1955).

Mary Adelle Beaverho and her son Joe, on her back, Lac La Martre (1955).

The children shown in this introduction are now adults or approaching adulthood. They were children of a time in history when traditional lifestyle practices known to their parents or grandparents were being significantly altered by an industrialized economy. Their ancestors' first shift from traditional practices was brought upon by the fur trade economy of the nineteenth century.

Some of the parents and most of the grandparents of these children knew and practised a quasi-bushland cultural lifestyle of hunting, gathering, and production of natural resources. In the years that these children were born, the fur trade industry was not a viable economy because fur had lost its value in the world's fashion market.

Some of these children retained traditional language capabilities; others did not. Many of the elements of the culture practised by their grandparents or parents are no longer practical. A lifestyle change from a culture that depended solely on the resources of the land to a culture that exploits that land for commercial purposes has been a transition fraught with the prospect of a total loss of traditional Aboriginal folkways. An industrialized society is the future for the children shown here, but there has not been a complete transition from traditional culture to industrial culture by some of the parents and grandparents shown in this book.

This book serves to bring to light, for everyone, the value of the knowledge and skills which were so important to the people who, for thousands of years, lived solely from the resources of the land. This book attempts to honour the knowledge of the people and the heritage they represent.

Opposite page: Stanley Houle, Bennith Houle, Darlene Nanemahoo, Darren Houle, and Anne Star (Peerless Lake, 1988).

Camp and home lifestyle

"OUR CAMP"

People living on bush traplines call their home "camp", as in "Come to our camp" or "Tie your dogs at our camp". Of course, in the harsh climate of the boreal forest, shelter is essential, and a comfortable camp usually included a permanent, weatherproof home built from local timber.

BASE CAMP LOCATION

Every base camp home is built on a river or lake. Since there are few roads, water transportation is vital. Nowadays, access to sites is by power boats, snowmobiles and all-terrain pneumatic wheeled vehicles. Traditional Aboriginal house construction material included logs, sod, bark, moss for the main frame and roof, animal skins for doors and windows, and soil and boughs of evergreens for flooring. Advantage was taken of natural sheltered areas such as banks or contours of land and regions of heavy tree growth.

The modern bush person may still use logs, but it would be unusual to build exclusively with naturally occurring materials. If logs are found upstream from the camp, they can be floated to the building site. Lumber may be purchased from local sawmills, while hardware and glass are marketed in the larger communities. These materials are moved to the camp by boat or skiff.

SPACE

Home base is the primary camp where a trapping family spends most of its time. A base camp is often a single-room log home, of thirty to forty square metres (three-hundred-twenty-three square feet). The building may be expanded with the addition of a porch or veranda, or by adding extra rooms. In addition to the base camp, one or more line cabins may serve as temporary camps while the family is fishing, hunting, or trapping far from home.

CLEARING OPEN SPACE

Trees, shrubs, and tall grass are cleared away in the area around the home and in the space between the building and the shoreline. Clearing trees and brush from around the home reduces the risk of damage during forest fires. This clearing provides a sunny, open space suitable for a garden, an open-air fireplace, some drying racks, or a smoke tent for curing meat and fish. The clearing is also a work area, where boats can be built, docked, or stored; hides can be cleaned; and furs can be prepared for sale. Clearing this brush opens up the views to the transportation route on the lake or river. A few well-placed shade trees combined with cool breezes off the water help to control flies and bugs, making the yard a comfortable place to live and work.

DRAINAGE

It is important to build a home on a site located above the flood plain of a river or lake to allow for good drainage. High water levels are assessed by examining watermarks on trees, rock formations, and the banks of rivers and lakes. The highest water levels along rivers usually occur during the spring break-up of river ice, when ice-jams cause the water to back up. Later, in June, thc snow finally melts high in the mountains, contributing much of the water in northern drainages. These heavy run-offs cause water levels to rise, though not as dramatically as the ice-jams. The break-up and run-off occur at about the same time each year, but flood levels vary depending on the weather each winter.

Another predictable hazard is the high water levels caused by winds pushing the water towards the shore. Strong winds can raise water levels by as much as a metre on a large lake. Heavy rains may cause local flooding, and storms far upstream can cause floods miles away downstream. Bushland residents expect changes in water levels under such conditions, and choose their building sites accordingly.

EXPOSURE TO SUN

Building sites are carefully selected according to whether a family wants more sun in the morning or the evening, or in summer or winter. In northern latitudes, the sun is low in the southern sky all winter, while it appears in the northern sky during the summer. Accordingly, an east-west shoreline was usually preferred where a camp on the south side of the water provided longer hours of sunlight in the summer, or one on the north side welcomed the warming rays of the sun during the winter. A location on a peninsula could offer both a sunrise and sunset.

ACCESS TO FOOD

Nearby fishing, hunting, and trapping areas are all important considerations in the selection of a base campsite. The bush person is familiar with the spawning areas of fish and the feeding grounds favoured by numerous animals. Moose, for instance, are likely to be found in low-lying areas with new, succulent aspen and grasses, and not in mature evergreen forests. Meat for human consumption is mainly from cloven-hoofed animals (moose, caribou, deer) some fur-bearers (rabbit, squirrel, muskrat, beaver), birds, and fish. Porcupines and, occasionally, lynx are also eaten.

SHORELINES

Rivers have always been the highways of the bushlands. For ease of transportation, the home base residence is almost always located on the shore of a lake or river, often where tributaries join. These water transportation routes link the home base with those of other hunters and trappers, and with service communities. Lakes and rivers are convenient gathering points for social activities. During open water seasons, travel is by boat; in winter, ice-covered rivers and lakes are again convenient routes for water transportation. In the spring and fall, there are short periods in which the ice is unsafe, and bush people are forced to travel overland.

An ideal shoreline is sand or gravel that slopes gradually towards the water. Mud and loose sand are to be avoided because they are subject to erosion and are messy to work on when loading, unloading, and docking boats. Traditionally, the Dogrib people would only live on islands during the spring season due to the belief that a creature named Negaw made the mainland unsafe during that time.

TIMBER STAND

An ideal home base includes a nearby stand of timber with both dry (dead) and green (live) firewood. A good supply of logs, anywhere from seventy to eighty trees twenty to thirty centimetres (eight to twelve inches) in diameter, is needed to build a log home. It is most convenient if these trees are close enough to be dragged to the building site.

LOGS

Spruce trees are the preferred source of logs for house construction, though pine or poplar trees are sometimes used. Logs must be straight, eight to ten metres (twenty-six to thirty-three feet) long, and of consistent diameter over the length of the house. The live green logs will shrink for two or three years as the house dries. As the cabin will shrink up to ten centimetres (four inches), doors and windows are set into the walls but not nailed into place.

CONSTRUCTION PROCESS

Each tree is felled, branches are trimmed off, and the bark is removed. Logs are cut to the home's side-wall and end-wall lengths. After the actual construction, log ends are trimmed off and piled for later use as firewood. The builder sometimes cut, trimmed, and dressed the logs alone, but usually had help dragging logs into position, and stacking them one upon another to form the walls.

ROOF

The traditional roof for a log cabin is a series of poles about ten centimetres (four inches) in diameter, placed side by side to span the distance between the side walls and the ridgepole. This ridgepole, which forms the peak of the roof, is about one metre (three-and-a-third feet) higher than the side walls, giving the roof a slope of about one-in-four. The ridgepole is supported by sloping logs resting on the corners of the walls, and reinforced by an upright supporting pole that stands atop the centre of the side wall. Large cabins, seven or eight metres (twenty-three to twenty-six feet) wide, will have secondary ridgepoles halfway between the overhang at the side walls and the peak.

On top of the poles, a layer of muskeg or peat moss (sphagnum) absorbs moisture from the inside of the cabin. The top layer of the roof is a cover of grassy sod, similar to the sod used on neighbourhood lawns. Sod deflects rain and snow, although traditional roofs made of all-natural materials do leak in prolonged, heavy storms. Modern cabin construction includes a mixture of logs and lumber, and usually uses commercial roofing materials.

DOORS AND WINDOWS

Before glass was available, a window opening was covered by a thin layer of rawhide. A door was made from small, moosehide covered logs, and heavy moosehide was used for hinges. Nowadays, commercially made doors and windows are typical. Because log walls shrink or settle for two or three years, windows and doors are loosely set in openings taller than the height of the window or door frame. While the home shrinks to its final height, these gaps are filled with insulation.

FLOOR

It is rare now to see a home with a dirt floor, and such cabins are typically used only as overnight accommodation by trappers. Dirt floors are covered with long grass or spruce boughs. The floor is cleaned by burning the grass and boughs and replacing them with fresh material.

CHINKING

Chinking is a mix of mud and a suitable fibre such as moss or moose hair. Gaps between the walls of a log cabin are filled with this caulking compound to prevent drafts. If the logs forming the cabin walls are of a particularly large diameter, the chinking may be overlaid by smaller poles.

WHITEWASH

Whitewash is made from limestone, shale, or white soil found in outcroppings along river banks. Whitewash is manufactured by heating these minerals, which disintegrate into a powder. They are usually heated in a stone oven dug into the earth, right where suitable minerals are found. A wood fire is prepared, and the burning logs are transferred into the oven when they are as hot as possible. The logs are placed both above and below the stone to generate intense heat. After the powder has cooled, it is strained to separate it from the ashes, and then mixed with fine sand and water. This grayish or off-white liquid is applied to the logs of a building, both to decorate and to preserve the wood (Zachary Powder, Fort McKay, 1970s; "Old" Julian Nanemahoo, Trout Lake; Lucy Cardinal, Wabasca-Desmarais, and many others, 1995).

SEATING

As recently as the 1960s, there were elderly bush people who had never used a chair. Traditionally, people ate, slept, worked, and relaxed while sitting, lying, or kneeling on the floor. In public places such as churches, these Elders would sit on the floor, and not in a pew. At some traditional bush camps, such as those used in the spring fishing season, and when muskrat hunting, Elders still prefer to sit on the ground. In traditional camps, bush people sleep on bedrolls laid over a mattress of spruce boughs. The mattress cover may be an animal hide with the fur left on.

LINE CABINS

When dog-team or walking is the only means of travel, a trapper could only cover about twenty kilometres (twelve-and-a-quarter miles) per day while checking sets (traps). Thus, at about twenty kilometre intervals, smaller line cabins were built to provide overnight shelter. Modern transportation along the trapline is often by snowmobile or all-terrain vehicle, allowing for longer distances between line cabins.

FABRIC SHELTERS

Tents served as portable trapline homes which were carried from camp to camp. Traditionally, tents were made from the hides of moose or other large animals, but more recently, fabric tents have been used, especially for the spring and summer fishing camps. Tents are also used in the winter. In the 1950s, most Dogrib hunters and trappers in the Northwest Territories lived in canvas wall tents for months each winter, while away from their log homes in the main settlements.

Tents vary in size, but are typically about three metres by four metres (nine to thirteen feet), with a one metre (three-and-a-third foot) side wall. In winter, the outside walls are banked with snow. Before the tent is set up, snow is removed from the floor area, and it is covered with spruce boughs, canvas, blankets, or hides. A stove will keep the tent warm in the coldest weather, but temperatures inside cool off quickly as the fire subsides. For this reason, bush people will often sleep within reach of kindling, so they can start a fire in the stove before they get out of bed in the morning!

FOOD CACHES AND EQUIPMENT SHELTERS

A food cache is a place where food is stored out of reach of animals. Caches are built at strategic locations along traplines and hunting routes, and at line cabins. A simple cache may be a bundle of supplies hung in a tree out of reach of animals, or a cache can be a permanent shed built of heavy logs to keep out bears, and sealed to prevent the entrance of smaller scavengers such as birds.

A permanent structure may be one or two metres (three-and-a-third to six-and-two-thirds feet) high and two metres square (twenty-one-and-a-half square feet), constructed of logs up to thirty centimetres (eleven-and-three-quarter inches) in diameter. The ground is covered with logs or branches, and the top is layered with poles. The entrance may be protected by loose, heavy logs, but by a permanent, hinged door at regularly used camps.

Shelters which house traps, tools, toboggans, and other non-perishable supplies do not require such elaborate precautions against animals, so these log sheds are not so tightly enclosed. Many trapping and hunting Elders will know of this practice, or will have built and used food caches themselves (1995).

DECOMPOSITION

Trapline cabins eventually wear out. Over time, the natural resin in the logs is replaced by water, which freezes and thaws, gradually expanding cracks and eventually splitting and rotting the wood. A well-built cabin will last the lifetime of the builder, but succeeding generations may need to build a new house from fresh logs, a process which is easier than repairing and replacing logs one by one. Old logs eventually decompose, leaving only a faint depression or a vague outline on the ground to show where a comfortable home once stood.

BURIAL

Family members, friends, and ancestors of the people pictured in this book are buried near traditional bushland homes, and along abandoned trails. Many graves are marked only by trees, shrubs, and grasses. The grave sites illustrated in this book are also gradually being overgrown. While they may be difficult to see, they remain family and community landmarks, now vulnerable to unsuspecting industrial development, and increasing recreational use.

SERVICE COMMUNITIES

Most trappers and hunters have now switched their home base from the trapline to a larger, centrally located community which offers shopping, business, schools, and health and social services. Examples of such towns are Fort Chipewyan (Alberta), or Rae-Edzo (Northwest Territories). Here, the people of the bushland have easy access to services, living in homes equipped with power, water, sewage, and telephones.

The access to schools and jobs which the towns provided encouraged the switch from full-time living on traplines to a community lifestyle. This transition is recent: At Fort Rae from 1955 to 1956, only six children out of a community of eight hundred attended school. At that time, trappers and their families travelled to trapline homes and remained there most of the year, except for Christmas, Easter, and the summer months, when they returned to Fort Rae to market their furs, buy supplies, and visit with friends and relatives. During this period in the bush, children learned and experienced the culture of a bush economy. Since then, school, followed by the promise of cash incomes away from the trapline, has drawn many members of younger generations out of the bush and into an urban lifestyle. In the year 2001, this same community graduated several students out of senior high school.

For thousands of years, people hunted and trapped on this land, living off resources renewed every year by nature. But now, François Orr's trapline has literally been cleared away to make way for oil sands development. Non-renewable resources have far greater immediate value in a modern, industrial culture.

François Orr in front of his home base trapline cabin (near Fort McKay, 1978).

Above: François Orr's home base storage shelter. This canvas tent is a warehouse for equipment, hardware supplies, and frozen or dried food which is hung on the ridgepole (or rope), out of reach of small fur animals and rodents in the winter. In the summer this shelter would not contain unsecured food – it could be raided by a bear.

Right: A line cabin site, located forty kilometres (twenty-five miles) from the home base, accommodated François Orr and his family for a few days at a time. Oil sands development is now in its place (near Fort McKay, March, 1978).

Above: François Orr, shaking snow off his equipment at his trapline cabin.

Left: François Orr, on his trapline near Fort McKay. He is checking his beaver trap set (March 1978).

Toboggans hitched to be pulled by a snowmobile (Garden Creek, Wood Buffalo Park, 1989).

Tethered to stakes for the summer months, sleigh dogs subsist on a regular diet of raw fish and plenty of water. By 1980, it was rare to find trappers with a full complement of dogs for winter travel (Mile 173, Athabasca River, south of Fort Chipewyan, 1980).

Occasionally, a wolf will mate with a female sleigh dog, resulting in hybrid wolf dog offspring, Wolf dogs are claimed by trappers to have the playful and active disposition of wolves, but this aspect of wolf dogs can make them difficult to train as sleigh dogs; their restless nature can make them less inclined to pay attention to the business of pulling a toboggan. This wolf dog was tethered in the dog-team line of Archie and Noreen Cardinal (Mile 156, Athabasca River, 1977).

A dog harness, set aside for the summer, is hung on a tree branch.

Top: Julian Nanemahoo has stored his snowshoes in tall willows for the summer (Gods Lake, September 1995).

Above left: A dog harness stored on the corner pole of a cabin.

Above right: Steel trap hung in a tree for storage and safe keeping.

An ice pick (left) and a small mammal steel trap (right). There are many tools and implements which may be left at a trapline cabin in the summer while the trapper is away. Traditional life did not include locking any building or securing tools and implements where they could not be seen by a visitor.

Top left: Traps are often partially enclosed by sticks or poles, so that animals drawn to the bait are forced to approach it over the trap. Traps may be left in place through the summer, ready for use the following trapping season (Willy Grandjambe trapline, Moose Lake).

Left: An enclosure made of smaller branches, seen during the trapping season.

Above: Julian Nanemahoo at his trapline (Gods Lake, September 1995).

Julian Nanemahoo peers through the window of his trapline cabin. Built for short-term use, a cabin will stand for many years in Alberta's relatively dry climate. This is a short-term cabin, as evidenced by the old-style sod roof, and the logs which have not yet been stripped of bark or trimmed at the corners of the building. Logs with bark will deteriorate more quickly than peeled logs, and sod needs regular, almost yearly, maintenance. Except for door hinges and window covers, construction products come from the land in the immediate area (Gods Lake, September 1995).

In the days of hunting and gathering, Aboriginal people buried their dead where they lived. Several graves are at this site on Julian's trapline. The last burials here took place in the 1920s.

Moss and mud are mixed together as chinking to fill the gaps between logs (Calling River, 1995).

Detail of pole and sod roof on an abandoned building. These poles are as much as fifteen centimetres (six inches) in diameter, and the sod is about fifteen centimetres deep. When soaked by rain, such deep sod becomes very heavy. The hand hewn stake in the second pole helps secure the pole to the frame of the building (Calling River, September 1995).

This trapline cabin has a sod roof. The porch or entrance to this building is constructed with vertical logs. Placing logs upright is not a standard construction model, but it suits small buildings such as the outhouse pictured at right (Archie Burke trapline, Fort Fitzgerald, 1980).

Opposite page: The home of Emily Champagne and George Wanderingspirit was built with logs, but the door, roof cover, and windows were commercially purchased. This is traditional construction influenced by traded produce introduced in the eighteenth century by the fur trade industry (Slave River, north of Fort Chipewyan).

Noreen and Archie Cardinal built this home from lumber produced by a friend at a nearby two-person sawmill. The Cardinals previously lived in a log built home at Mile 156 of the Athabasca River, twenty-nine kilometres (eighteen miles) south of this location. This trapline home advances the use of building technology, including four rooms, a propane cooking stove, a wood heating stove, an asphalt shingle roof, and more glass window space than is usual for a log home – in all, more comforts than the Cardinals were accustomed to in their previous log home. Still, this modern home is on their trapline, several miles from their neighbours (1966).

This shelter is for tools and equipment. This style of structure could also function as a dog shelter or a small meat curing smokehouse (Archie Burke, Fort Fitzgerald, 1980).

Above: George Noskiye was eighty-eight years old at the time this photo was taken (1995).

Left: A canvas tent has many uses in the bush. It can be a year-round or temporary residence, a shelter for curing meat and fish, or a shelter for equipment and supplies (Christine and George Noskiye, Trout Lake, 1995).

Alphonse Beaver was aged ninety-six at the time this photograph was taken. Alphonse, an accomplished craftsman, built this canoe by hewing and moulding the boards with hand tools from a tree he collected nearby (Sandy Lake, 1995).

Top left and right: This handcrafted canoe has aged and will not likely see water again. It may stay stored where it is until it is weathered to bits or until it is broken up for firewood (1995).

Traditional tents were circular, while canvas tents introduced during the Fur Trade era are rectangular. Many rectangular tents, like the one shown here, are popular as temporary or seasonal residences of people who live in the bush for extended periods, like the trapping season.

Wooden smokehouse of the type occasionally found in the central northeast region of Alberta. This style of smokehouse, built from locally available material, has now been replaced in most regions by an easily assembled conical tent of canvas (Adele Gladue, Wabasca-Desmarais, 1995).

Opposite page: A conical tent smokehouse to smoke-cure fish or other meat (Jean D'or Prairie, 1989).

Sweat Lodge and The Sweat

Sweats are common to many Aboriginal cultures. It is a way to contemplate one's spiritual and physical well-being and, if one wishes, share that contemplation with others. The primary function of a Sweat is to have a spiritual experience that is a source of strength, healing, and direction in a very personal way. The Sweat Lodge is the place to do that.

This is a description of the process nvolved with a Sweat, as described by Raymond Cardinal, Clarence Cardinal, and François Auger-Cardinal. It is reported here with their concurrence. Typically, a Sweat is for both men and women using a common Sweat Lodge, but Sweats may be exclusively men or women in separate Lodges. This exclusive tradition, seldom practised, is reflected in the construction of a men's Lodge built with one hundred forty-five willow branches, and a women's Lodge built with sixty-five willow branches. Where this story takes place there is a third, symbolic Lodge for the bear. Although there are three Lodges, only one Lodge is used, concurrently by both men and women.

The traditional Lodge is dome-shaped and made with willow branches. Each branch is placed on the ground and bent to the centre of the dome. The Lodge is round, not high enough to stand in, and not normally more than three or four metres (ten to thirteen feet) across the floor. Lodges are owned by one or more persons; in this example three people own the Lodge. The Lodge owner may also be the doorkeeper during the Sweat Ceremony. The doorkeeper's responsibility is to prepare the Lodge, welcome guests, and heat stones on a fire outside of the Lodge. Stones are picked from a shoreline. The Sweat Lodge owner will know how many stones should be heated. A container of water is placed inside the lodge, close to where the hot stones will be placed.

Participants wear light clothing; no one will wear jewellery or ornaments. They enter and sit on the ground encircling the heated rock. They bring a modest gift of beads, or berries, or kinnickinnick (tobacco), or virtually anything that is represented as an Offering. The Offering does not have to be anything elaborate – it's the meaning that counts. In this Sweat, a carved human facial image was located at the entrance to the Lodge. These images are carved into a log taken from the trunk of a birch tree. The log is two metres (six-and-a-half feet) high

A Sweat Lodge frame made of bent willow branches. Although traditional Sweats were rare for several decades, they are again a common spiritual practice in many communities (Wabasca-Desmarais, 1995).

and fifteen centimetres (six inches) wide, and stands upright with the carving at the very top. The head of this image is covered with the feathered skin of a grouse. It is at this sacred image that Offerings are customarily presented.

When the stones are red-hot, they are moved from the outside fire pit to the centre of the Lodge and placed in a hole in the ground that was previously sprinkled with a handful of fungus or sweet-grass. There should not be any dust or ashes on the stones. Herbs, usually wolf-willow leaves, are placed on the stones to create a natural, pleasant plant aroma which filters through the Lodge.

The Lodge owner will conduct a Sweet-grass or Pipe Ritual, blessing the people, the rocks, and the event. Each person may, and usually does, conduct their own blessing, each in their own way and for their particular reasons. Braided sweetgrass or a clump of fungus will be set afire, to smoulder and emit smoke, acting as a pipe if an actual pipe is not being used. A fresh willow branch with leaves is used to take water from a container and sprinkle droplets over the hot stones, causing steam to circulate within the Lodge. As the steam rises, as the aroma of the wolf-willow and the sweet-grass circulates, the people pray and pass the smouldering fungus, sweet-grass, or pipe from one person to the next. A puff is taken from the pipe, or the essence of the sweet-grass or fungus is cupped in the participant's hand and spread over the head.

The Sweet-grass or Pipe Ceremony takes about fifteen minutes. During that time the Sweat Lodge holder will sing four spiritual songs. The participants may sing as well, or they may take turns singing the same song the Sweat Lodge owner has sung. This is one round of a Sweat. The Lodge door is opened and a participant may leave if he or she so wishes. During the Sweat, the Sweet-grass or Pipe Ceremony is repeated four times, fifteen minutes each time. Cooled stones are replaced with hot stones. The original container of water will be used by the end of the Sweat. The ash that remains from the wolf-willow, the fungus, and the sweet-grass becomes the property of the Lodge owner, who will later use it as a medicine to heal physical and mental illness, as a symbol of forgiveness to make amends for past deeds, or as a symbolic Offering to the Creator.

Sweat Lodge at Calling Lake (Winter, 1996).

Opposite page: A carved image stands at the entrance to a Sweat Lodge. This image is carved into a birch log which stands two metres (six-and-a-half feet) and is fifteen centimetres (six inches) in diameter. Grouse feathers are the head gear (Calling Lake, 1995).

Above and right: Additional angles of the image shown on the previous page. The hide and feathers of a grouse, shaped over the carving, act as a hairpiece.

Above: Raymond Cardinal – Sweat Lodge facilitator.

Right: François Auger-Cardinal, an Elder, narrated the description of the Sweat Lodge on the preceding pages. He and Raymond Cardinal, the Sweat Lodge facilitator, gave permission to have the Sweat Ceremony written and published. Their wish is that the publication will help ensure that the knowledge of this traditional practice will be preserved (Calling Lake, 1996).

A stone-walled oven is built in a bank, and used to bake limestone and shale to the consistency of powder. Only the oldest Aboriginal people retain the knowledge of this traditional practice, abandoned in the mid-1900s. This oven has not been used for burning limestone and shale since the 1930s. Burning limestone produces powdered lime which, when mixed with water, is a whitewash for log buildings. Powdered lime mixed in food or water is a medicine fed to a dog to eradicate tapeworm, a parasite that invades the intestine (Trout Lake, 1995).

An outcropping of shale along the banks of the Athabasca River. This outcrop contains limestone that yields powdered lime when burned (1961).

Above: This is a raised fireplace built with logs and filled with earth. The perimeter of the box is cleared of vegetation to prevent the spread of fire to the pine needles, leaves, twigs, dried plants, and dried wood on the forest floor (Wabasca-Desmarais, 1995).

Opposite page: This is a log building painted with locally produced whitewash (Chipewyan Lakes, 1995).

A wood chopping block. Two poles, two metres (six-and- a-half feet) long, are attached vertically, about fifteen centimetres (six inches) apart, to a tree stump. Logs to be cut are held in place between the poles so that both hands are free to saw or swing an axe. This safety measure reduces potential injury by preventing a log from moving while being cut (James "Jimmy" Donavan, Anzac, 1993).

Above: Wood may continue to be useful even after it has been used to heat a cabin or cook food. Wood ash is an ingredient used in the production of soap. Charcoal is a tool to sketch a design on fabric on which hair will be tufted, and porcupine quill or fish scale will be artistically applied.

Left: Decomposed wood is used by boreal forest people for tanning hides.

Above: For centuries, wood was the sole fuel used by the bushland people. This wood, cut to stove or heater size, is stacked ready for use.

Right: A firewood drying rack. Poles exposed to the sun are set teepee style, to allow dry air to circulate. This is an effective way to dry freshly-cut wood, and to keep dry wood off the damp ground. This system is also used to dry poles for fencing, teepees, and general construction.

Left: Teepee poles are selected for uniform length and thickness. They are stored upright to protect them from moisture, and will be moved to wherever the teepee is needed (Katy Sanderson, Fort McMurray, 1993).

Below: This appears to be a teepee frame. Logs are propped with the narrow end up, to be dried by sun and wind. Logs this length may be for the construction of a pole fence, or may be cut for household firewood (Fort Fitzgerald, 1980).

Below: Shallow streams are often places for temporary storage and refrigeration of food. This upper stream is edged with the early frost of fall; the lower stream is as it would be seen in the summer.

Water for drinking and cooking is taken from streams, rivers, or lakes. If no surface water is available, a small hole dug into the muskeg will usually fill with water. A traditional belief was that if bugs were in the water, it was safe to use; water with no bugs was likely to be contaminated with subsurface minerals.

Top: Snow, lake, and river ice and icicles hanging from shoreline trees are sources of water (François Auger-Cardinal, Orloff Lake, 1996).

Above: Charles Peter Nitsiza is drinking water from a lake (Fort Rae, Northwest Territories, August 1955).

A natural cooler. A large tree is cut off about a metre (three-and-a-quarter feet) above the ground. The stump is then hollowed out to within five centimetres (two inches) of the bark. This cavity extends down to the roots and the cool earth around them where lard will stay firm even in the hottest days of summer. Ground cover provides insulation and the cooler is covered to keep out sun, rodents, and flies. The above ground portion of the cooler, when covered, is scavenger-proof storage for produce which does not need to be kept cool (Archie and Noreen Cardinal trapline at Mile 156, Athabasca River, Fort Chipweyan, 1978).

Top row from left to right: These cooking containers are hanging from trees and shrubs at abandoned trapline sites along the Athabasca River. This style of metal cooking pot followed the copper pots that were introduced to the Aboriginal peoples when Europeans traded for fur. Traditional containers were made from resources of the land (north of Fort McMurray, 1995).

Above right: The stump of a tree is used as a seat, a small table, or a place to rest a tea pail (Archie and Noreen Cardinal trapline at Mile 156, Athabasca River, Fort Chipewyan, 1978).

Left: A metal pail, such as this tea pail, is often the only cooking container on a trapping and hunting trip. A metal grate is available at main camps, but on the trail, green branches will serve the same purpose.

Above: Smoke cured fish, dried and ready to eat, hangs on a pole over the campfire.

Opposite page: Drying racks at a Dogrib community at the south end of Marian Lake. The fish seen here is prepared for human consumption (south of Fort Rae, 1955).

Opposite page insert: Fish fillets showing the parallel cuts which expose the flesh to heat, air, and smoke. (Elise Lepine, Madeline Whiteknife, Fort Chipewyan, 1980).

Top right: These racks are a framework of narrow poles at least two metres (six-and-a-half feet) above the ground. Fish or meat is hung over the poles to dry in the sun. A simmering fire below the rack will provide a trickle of smoke which helps to cure (preserve) the meat (1995).

Fishing nets at an Orloff Lake fishing camp. Nets are removed from the water, and hung to dry. If the nets are left in the water, the constant moisture and rotting of unwanted dead fish will cause the mesh to deteriorate. While they are in the water, the nets are checked every day, and as soon as enough fish are caught, the net is taken out. Nets require regular maintenance, to fix tears in the mesh (François Auger-Cardinal, Calling Lake, 1995).

Above: Elise Lepine at spring camp for fish preparation and muskrat hunting (Fort Chipewyan, 1980).

Above right: Elise Lepine, Madeline Whiteknife, and Louie Martin have a tea break with visitors to their spring fishing camp.

Right: Madeline Whiteknife at spring camp (Fort Chipewyan, 1980).

Opposite page: Louie Martin of Fort Chipewyan at spring fishing camp. Traditional lifestyle did not include tables and chairs, so it was not unusual to find elderly people seated on the ground for relaxation, for eating, and for working at jobs which could be done by hand, such as preparing food and pelts (1980).

Left: Michel Bouvier. Mr. Bouvier was sixty-four when this photo was taken. He was fluent in Dogrib, Chipewyan, English, and French, and worked as a translator for the Dogrib people of Fort Rae, assisting them in dealings with doctors, the RCMP, and the government. In 1918, he was recruited by the Canadian Army to serve as a dog musher in Siberia. He reported to Calgary for military training, but the war ended before his service was required (Fort Rae, 1955).

Top: Marie Bouvier preparing to cure whitefish. Note the special way this fish is cut: the sides and belly are in one piece while a narrow strip, formed with a cut along each side of the spine, is connected at the tail and hangs over the pole (Fort Rae, 1956).

Above: The spring fishing camp of Michel and Marie Bouvier (Fort Rae, 1955).

Raymond Cardinal of Calling Lake is hanging this moose hindquarter from a tree branch at the camp of John and Mabel Bigstone. The moose meat will dry, forming a hard outer crust. Beneath this outer layer, the meat will tenderize and remain fresh.

Eventually, the meat would dry completely, but usually it is consumed long before going to waste. Cuts are taken as needed. The fresh meat is cooked, and the outer crust is used to bait traps, or to feed dogs (1995).

Top right: Moose ribs being smoke cured over a smouldering fire (John and Mabel Bigstone, Calling Lake, 1995).

Right: This moose meat has been dried, pulverized, and mixed with berries and fat. It is a modern form of pemmican, a mainstay food supply of the fur trade era when buffalo was the source of meat.

Above: This three to four kilogram (six to eight pound) piece of moose meat is being cured on a rack made of green willow sticks, about one metre (three-and-a-quarter feet) above a smouldering fire. Preparation began by cutting a slice about one centimetre (two-fifths of an inch) thick while avoiding cutting all the way through the meat. The next slice came in from the other side, parallel to the first, and slices were alternated again so that the original chunk of meat could be unfolded in a long piece about one centimetre thick. Slicing the meat in this manner keeps it in one piece, but allows the heat and smoke from the fire to reach the inner portions of the chunk so that it can be cured all the way through.

Above: Moose meat is cured by warm air and smoke. It may be eaten dry or boiled. Cured, finely-minced meat is mixed with fat and berries to make pemmican (Noreen and Archie Cardinal, Mile 156, Athabasca River, Fort Chipewyan).

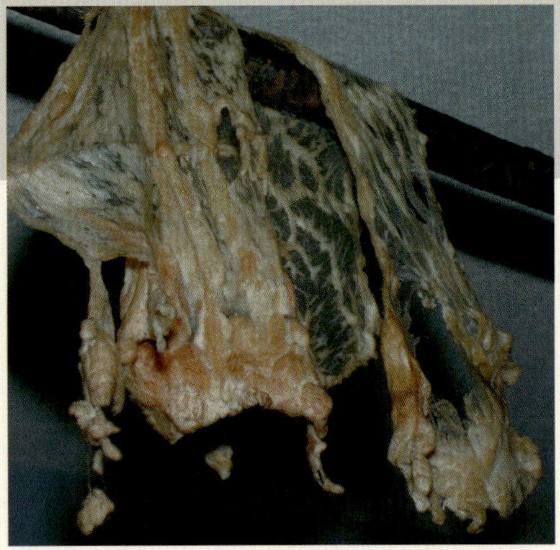

Right: Crackling is made from the cape which surrounds the stomach of a moose. The fat is rendered out, leaving the remaining fibre which is cooked until crisp. This tasty snack is sometimes referred to as "Indian popcorn" (James Grandjambe and others, Fort McKay, 1994).

Opposite page: Whole fish, for the dogs. Several fish, weighing about nine kilograms (twenty pounds) each, are hung on a stick to dry and preserve. Dried fish are much lighter than frozen or fresh fish, but retain the same nutritional value.

Opposite page insert: Whole fish are being dried for use as dog food (Joe Punch, Samba K'e [Trout Lake], 1994).

Hanging from the drying rack or in a nearby bush, a dead bird may be used as a scarecrow. As the bird carcass rots, it may also be used as bait in a trap to catch small fur-bearing animals. A dead raven is perched nearby to scare off scavenging ravens (Joe Punch, Samba K'e [Trout Lake], 1994).

The skin of a large northern pike, which will be used to bait traps, hangs alongside a whole whitefish (Joe Punch, Samba K'e [Trout Lake], 1994).

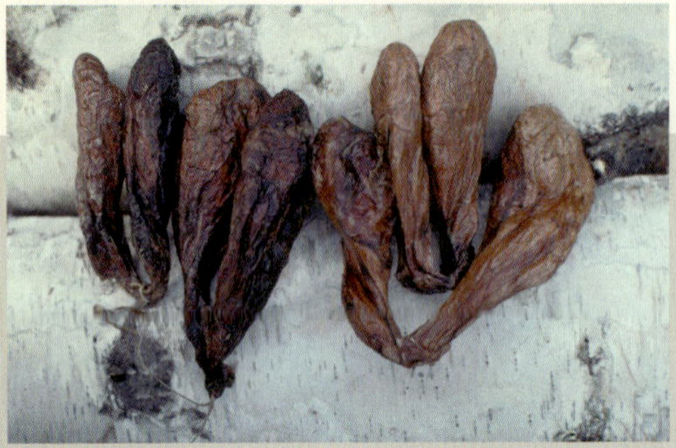

Right: Four sets of castor glands. Each beaver has one such pair (Katy Sanderson, Fort McMurray, 1993).

Above: A beaver carcass is slowly baked over an open fire. Beaver is also sliced and fried, or cut into chunks and stewed (Katy Sanderson, Fort McMurray, 1993).

Left: Katy Sanderson preparing a beaver pelt. In this case, the pelt is stretched and nailed onto a flat, wooden surface. Another method is to form a wooden hoop and stretch the hide by lacing it to the hoop; this is a small scale version of the moose-hide stretchers visible in the background of this photo. No matter how the beaver pelt is stretched, it is then cleaned of all fat and meat and cured or tanned with the hair left on. This was the basic currency of the boreal forest during the heyday of the fur trade.

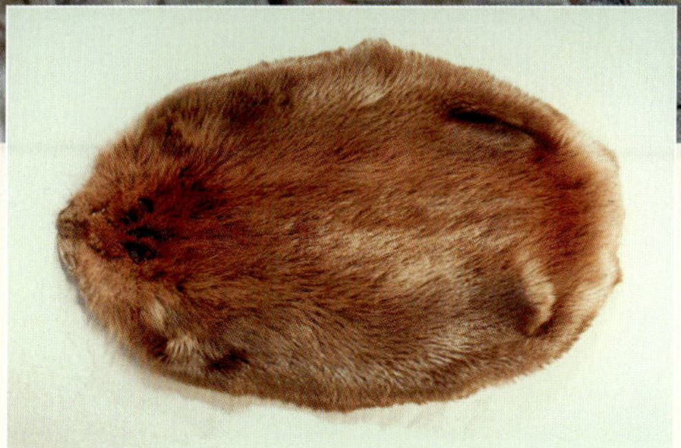

Above: Katy Sanderson views pelts of beaver, fox, wolf, and coyote. Such furs were once the traditional source of material for clothing in the bushlands. Now they are more likely to be sold for cash, and will eventually be sold in the fashionable shops of cities in North America, Europe, or Asia (Fort McMurray, 1994).

Right: A beaver pelt cushion. A cloth backing has been sewn to the outer edge of the pelt, and the resulting pouch is stuffed with moss, hair, or feathers.

Left: This trapline cabin has been abandoned since circa 1955. Weather will reduce it to an outline on the ground.

Below: Katy Sanderson and her husband George used this two metre by two-and-a-half metre (six foot by eight foot) cabin as a stopover for years. In the late 1970s, it was burned to the ground by unknown arsonists, the result of it being accessible to people who were not trappers of the area.

Above: This corner of a log house used as a temporary shelter illustrates a quick means of construction. These logs, placed one above the other with minimal axe work, are not weatherproofed as well as the logs prepared for the construction of a homebase cabin. Left without maintenance, this cabin will disintegrate over a period of about forty years.

Above: A birchbark shingle will, like the roof of the crumbling building it served, deteriorate over time (Mile 52, Athabasca River, north of Fort McKay, 1994).

Above centre: This chimney, built with wood, juts from the side of a home constructed with logs (Maryanne and Felix Beaver, Athabasca River, 1994).

Left: These homes are designed to stand for decades. Regular maintenance is required to replace chinking that deteriorates or falls away. Freezing and thawing may also damage chinking or cause logs to split, making occasional repairs necessary.

Opposite page: In the days before logs were sawed into lumber, the floors of cabins were covered with spruce boughs, long grass, or animal hides. Spruce boughs or sweetgrass each provided a pleasant aroma. Floors were cleaned by replacing these materials. This abandoned trapline cabin was destroyed a few days after the photo was taken to make way for a highway between Slave Lake and Wabasca (Fall, 1988).

Log cabins always have gaps between the logs. These gaps are filled or "chinked" with a caulking compound, which is a mixture of mud and one or more types of fibre. Examples of suitable fibres are moss, grass, or animal hair.

Left: A drying rack made of poles is strung over the kitchen cook stove. Racks are used to dry clothing, fur, or meat (Alice Boucher, Fort McKay, 1994).

Right: Poles make up the frame of a bunk bed. Spruce boughs, long grass, or fur hides will be used as a mattress (Willy Grandjambe, Moose Lake, 1994).

Raphael Cree, aged one-hundred-and-one, in Fort McMurray (1994).

Raphael and Louise Cree at their home, along the Clearwater River. Both Raphael and Louise were older than the province of Alberta; he was born in 1893, and she in 1899. Louise died in 1996, aged ninety-seven. Raphael lived in relatively good health until his death in 2002 at age one-hundred-and-eight. He lived in three centuries, and served as an active and reliable source of traditional knowledge (1977).

Photographed in 1961, this abandoned cabin along the Athabasca River south of Fort Chipewyan is all that remains of a small community of people. In time, this cabin will either disintegrate following years of exposure to rain, snow, wind, and frost, or it will fall over the eroding river bank and be swept in pieces downstream.

Old cabin sites are naturally recycled as new forest vegetation grows in. This barely visible log was once the base of a cabin (along the Athabasca River, south of Fort Chipewyan, 1994).

Grave marker made of stone, split and shaped by hand (northern Alberta, 1995).

Natural stone grave marker (northern Alberta, 1995).

Above: This unmarked grave is the burial site of three people. Memories are all that remain in this dense overgrowth of trees and shrubs, which was once the home area of Native trappers and hunters. It was a ray of sun shining through the trees that helped identify this site (Athabasca River, near Wood Buffalo Park, 1995).

Opposite page: This burial site is covered with new vegetation. A birch tree is protruding from one grave (Trout Lake, 1980).

Above left: Gravesite marker engraved with Cree language syllabics. There are several human remains at this site, all buried before 1922 (northeast Alberta, 1994).

Above: It is a traditional practice to leave an offering at the burial site to the memory of the person buried. The offering, known as kinnickinnick, is a natural form of tobacco, although in recent years it is not uncommon to offer commericially purchased tobacco. Julian Nanemahoo is pictured holding an offering to a family member and getting ready to return it to its rightful place. There has not been a person buried at this site since the 1930s (Gods Lake, 1995).

These grave marker poles are placed in the ground and tied together with a strip of bark. Note the lichen growth. These markers were placed before 1920 (Moose Lake, July 1994).

Some burial sites are fenced.

Willy Grandjambe, at the gravesite of his grandparents and sister, located along his trapline. They died at the same time in 1919. Their bodies were placed in a small log cabin at this location. Except for a faint outline of the cabin on the ground, this cross is their only visible memorial (1995).

Much of the transition from one-room log homes to modern homes in settlements has happened in the time period from the mid-twentieth century onward. The trapline cabin pictured is furnished with a propane cooking stove, and wood is the source of heat. The homes in the lower right are occupied by people who trap and hunt and take casual industrial work, living in a community that has all utility services. Some of the people in this community have lived through three or four generations of housing. These homes are fully equipped and furnished with twentieth century technology. The people, however, are still gatherers and hunters at heart, and some, in practice.

Fort McKay, along the Athabasca River. This traditional trapping and hunting community is now fully serviced with roads, electricity, water, and sewer. The people who live here have their own administration, general store, school, and social service. From towns like this, many trappers commute to traplines where their ancestors lived year 'round in earlier times. Residents of Fort McKay often visit the larger city of Fort McMurray to shop, conduct business, or get access to social, health, and educational facilities (1995).

Forest

Seen from a distance, the green, dark forest of summer seems uniform. On closer examination, deciduous trees, conifers, and shrubs each have their own unique hues. Look closer still, and you will see brilliant flowers and succulent fruit. The forest, which at first glance seemed to be an evergreen wall, is composed of hundreds of plant species. Many of these plants served the bushland people as foods, medicines, and tools.

Subtle shades of green give way to garish reds and yellows as winter approaches. The leaves of deciduous trees change colours and fall to the ground, leaving branches bare. In the winter, trunks and branches are off-white, grey, and shades of brown, among the evergreen spruce. The sun, always low in the sky, occasionally catches the brilliant red twigs of a leafless shrub. Moose will eat these twigs in winter, while they wait for the tender new vegetation which sprouts in the spring.

The larch tree, also called tamarack or "Indian hardwood", is the only conifer in the region that drops its needles. In a blaze of glory, larch needles turn a brilliant gold a few days before falling.

CARRYING FIRE FROM PLACE TO PLACE

Before Europeans brought flint-and-steel (and later matches) the bushland people made fire by striking a flint against a stone, which created sparks used to ignite very dry bark or leaves. Two pieces of dry wood could also be rubbed together until friction caused one piece to ignite. Needless to say, both methods were time-consuming, and there was good reason to keep a fire burning once it was lit. As the people moved from camp to camp, they needed a way to carry their fire with them.

A certain fungus, a parasitic growth on trees which grows up to thirty centimeters (twelve inches) long, will smoulder for days after being lit. A piece of this fungus was used to carry fire to a new camp. At the destination, the slow-burning fungus was blown on to encourage a small flame, which was in turn used to light some tinder. The smoke from the smouldering fungus also served as an insect repellant, and is still occasionally used for this purpose today (George Sanderson, and many others, Fort McMurray, 1963).

Willow fungus is smaller than tree fungus. It grows on dry willow branches close to damp ground. This fungus is sometimes used as an air freshener because of its pleasant aroma, which one can detect when walking through a willow grove. A piece of this fungus can also be used as an applicator to treat exposed wounds. It is also used as a sponge which is saturated with hot water or hot oil and placed in the ear to relieve an earache.

BARK AND WOOD FOR SNOWSHOE, TOBOGGAN, AND BASKET CONSTRUCTION

Tree bark is easiest to remove from trees located close to water. An abundance of moisture through the roots and bark makes such trees more pliable and easier to work with than dry trees. Trees exposed to the wind have fewer knots and are more pliable than trees that grow in wind-sheltered areas (Fred MacDonald, and many others).

While most bush construction is made with spruce, certain things, like snowshoe frames and toboggan runners, must be made with straight-grained hardwoods. Birch is used, but larch (also known as tamarack, or "Indian hardwood") is the most durable. The grain of most larch trees is twisted, but occasionally a straight tree is found. A skilled toboggan builder will find a tree from which straight boards can be cut. Runners made from these boards will withstand rough, icy, or bumpy terrain.

FOOD FROM THE TREES

Birch tree sap is a favorite source of syrup. A two-week period each spring is the best time to tap the trees and extract the sap flowing in the trees' inner bark.

Trees are tapped by making a V-shaped cut about five millimetres (one-fifth of an inch) deep in the bark. A stick, inserted at the point of the V, acts as a spout. A container is hung below the stick to catch the sap flowing from the cut and along the stick to drip off the end. Nowadays, the container is a metal or plastic pail, but in earlier times, a pail would be fashioned out of birchbark. As much as fourteen litres (three gallons) of sap will drip from each tree. This is boiled down to three or four litres (two-thirds to one gallon) of syrup, which is sometimes flavoured or sweetened with wild berries. Nowadays, sugar is occasionally added. Red willow branches may be boiled with the sap to give the syrup a dark, maple syrup colour (James Grandjambe, Katherine Boucher, Zachary Powder, Victoria Boucher, Alice Boucher, Katy Sanderson, and many others; Fort McKay and Fort McMurray, 1994).

Across the boreal forest, there are as many as two-dozen plants that bear edible fruits and berries. Some plants, such as the black currant, red currant, and twisted stalk, are rare. Others are both plentiful and widespread. Cranberries (the high bush, low bush, and bog varieties), pin cherry, blueberry, chokecherry, raspberry, saskatoon, and rosehip are familiar to all bushland people.

Aboriginal Elders used these berries in many ways. Berries could be eaten raw, or preserved as jam, jelly, or syrup. Berries could also be easily preserved by drying. Dried fruit could be softened by cooking it in water, or mixed with ground dried meat and fat to make pemmican. Dried berries were also beaded to create necklaces, or attached to crafts and clothing as decorations. Berry juice was used as a dye in the production of art and craft items.

Fruit availability depends on growing conditions which vary from year to year. High bush fruit plants are vulnerable to spring frosts. Ground cover plants, like the blueberry and bog cranberry, are found in sandy soils, and are also affected by spring weather. Raspberries and rosehips are found in disturbed soils, such as those along roadways or in recently-burned areas. Rosehips and high bush cranberries remain on the plant through the winter, and can be picked through the cold season when their natural vitamin C is particularly valuable. Where berries were plentiful in one year, there may be few the next; people must search out the best places each year.

A number of plants are also used to make drinks. Mint grows wild on the banks of beaver dams. It can be dried and preserved, or put fresh into hot water. Either way, it makes a refreshing tea.

Tobacco, as we now know it, was introduced with the fur trade. Traditional tobacco, called kinnickinnick, was the leaf of the bearberry plant found in pine forests. Bearberry leaves, which turn red in the fall, were picked and dried in the sun, then smoked in pipes. The inner bark of red willow is also kinnickinnick when crushed, dried, and smoked. Because modern tobacco is expensive, it is sometimes stretched by mixing it with leaves of the red willow or bearberry (Annie Ducharme, Johnny Orr, and many others, Fort McKay, 1994).

As recently as the early 1900s, it was a traditional practice of many Aboriginal people to repay the land with a gift, in exchange for a harvest of berries or other produce. Kinnickinnick was commonly offered, though other possessions would do. This practice reflected a belief that a plant taken from the land would replace itself if people offered a gift in return (Zachary Powder, François Orr, and many others, Fort McKay).

Would you like to know what makes the tree sing?
The tone of the tree depends on:
How low or how tall it is,
How big or how small around it is,
How wet or dry it is,
and what the force of the wind is
to bend and sway it.
That is how we get music from the bush.

- Zachary Powder

Opposite page: On a calm, clear winter day, snow and hoarfrost whitens the branches of evergreens, poplars, and shrubs (northern Alberta, 1995).

A trapper's clear cut trail in the winter.

A clear cut trail to a trapper's cabin in the spring (1995).

Clearwater River, near the trapline home of Louise and Raphael Cree (east of Fort McMurray, summer 1965).

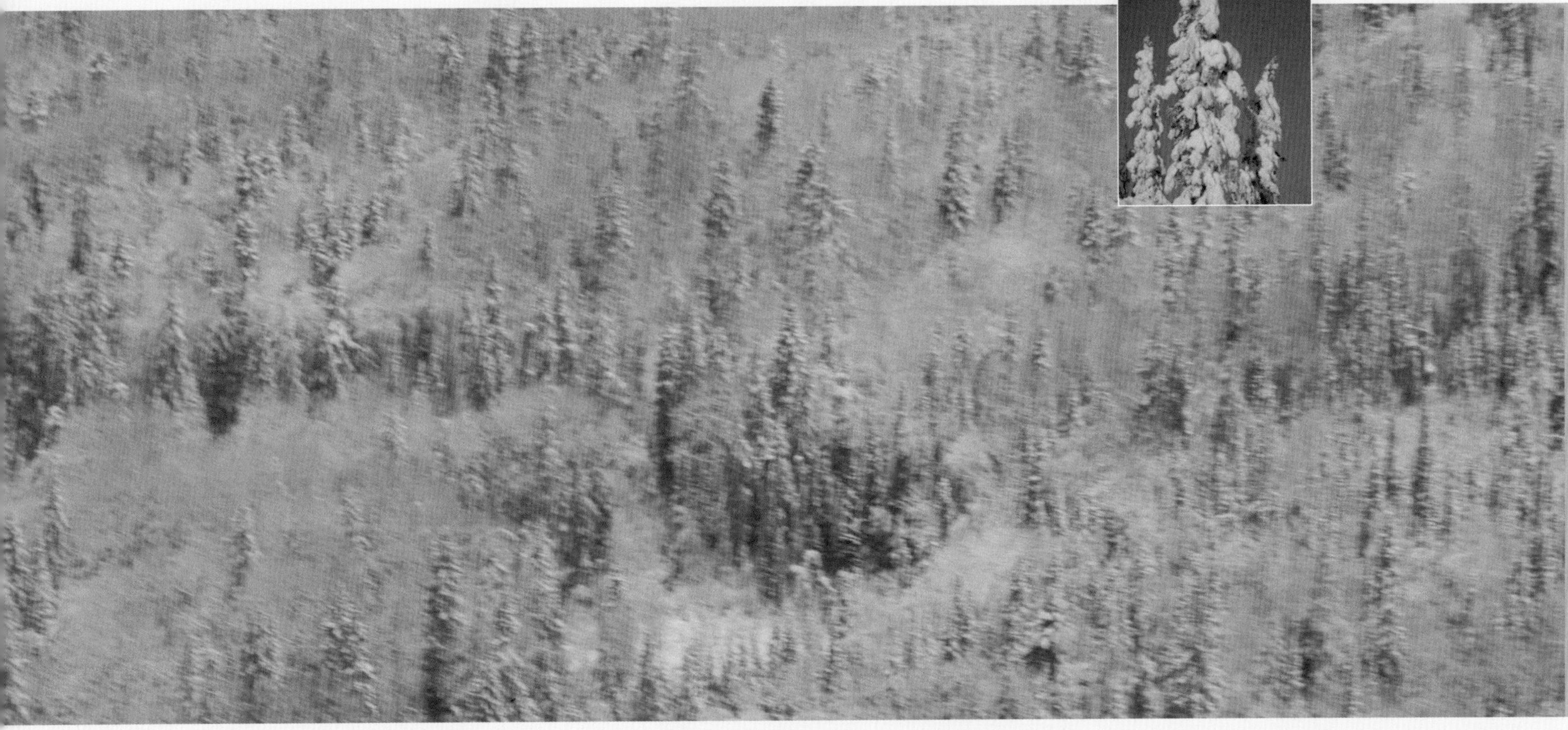

On a calm, clear winter day, snow and hoarfrost whitens the branches of evergreens, poplars, and shrubs (northern Alberta, 1995).

Above: Natural compass: In northwest Canada, the prevailing winds are from the northwest. Lichen growth is caused by moisture (rain and sleet) being blown on to the northwest face of a tree. The moisture drips to the base of the tree, providing nutrients for the lichen. This is a practical and natural compass for people travelling in the forest.

Right: Moss accumulates on the northwest side of a tree trunk as a result of wind forcing rain against the tree.

Fred MacDonald (above left). In 1942, when Fred was seven years old, his father planted this spruce tree (above) in memory of Fred's mother, who had died. This tree is on the bank of the Athabasca River, north of Fort McMurray (Fort McKay, 1994).

Opposite page: Fungus on a live birch tree.

Opposite page inserts: The smoke from a smouldering fungus is an effective insect repellent. – Fire lighter. Tree fungus of the type used to make a smouldering, flameless fire. When applied to kindling and blown, this fungus could be used to ignite a flame. In the days before matches, this was a practical way to transport fire between camps.

Tree fungus. There are many types of fungi, a plant in the same category as mushrooms, mildew, and mould. The size, type, and use of the fungus depends on the type of tree or shrub it grows on.

Willow fungus, as a medical sponge, absorbs warm water or oil, and one application is to place the heated sponge in the ear to relieve earache. As an air freshener, this fungus has a pleasant aroma that permeates the enclosed space of a log or fabric residence.

Above: This is a fallen tree at an advanced stage of decomposition. The decayed wood can be collected and used as an essential agent in the process of curing hides. Once set on fire, it slowly burns or smoulders, and billows smoke onto an overhanging hide. Smoke breaks down the fibres, causing the hide to soften and to turn a shade of brown.

Sap drips. These grooves cut in the trunk of a birch tree funnel sap to a container hanging from the tree. Sap seeps down the grooves, and onto a two-centimetre (two-thirds of an inch) stick, from which it drips into a container. It was thought, by the person who showed the way to this site, that sap had not been taken from these trees since the 1940s or 1950s (near Trout Lake, 1996).

Poplar trees produce a dark brown sap with a flavour similar to rhubarb. This sap is consumed like a soft drink (Victoria McDonald and others, Fort McKay, 1994) (Katy Sanderson, Fort McMurray, 1977).

The spruce tree produces a sticky gum used as a glue to stick the seams of crafts, and to seal cracks in baskets or canoes made of bark and wood.

Birds also leave their mark on trees. The yellow-bellied sapsucker and other woodpeckers nest in the cavities of trees. Sapsuckers tap orderly rows of small square pits through the bark of deciduous trees like the birch. The pits fill with sap which oozes from the green wood. The sapsucker visits the pits regularly to lap up the nutritious delicacy and to feast on insects attracted by the sap. This tree is pockmarked with hundreds of these pits. While the activity is essential to the survival of the birds, it may result in the death of affected trees, as the scars invite fungal diseases.

It is not unusual to see inscriptions on trees near campsites or trails. Like urban graffiti, these marks apparently have no particular meaning except to say, "I was here" (Moose Lake, 1994).

This anthill in a southern Alberta forest region illustrates the anthill's potential as a trap enclosure. Each of these hills is approximately one and one-half metres (five feet) high and one and one-half metres in diameter.

Ants can build structures as large as a cubic metre (ten and three-quarter square feet) or more. A trapper will turn this hill into a trap enclosure by burrowing an entrance at ground level and removing the centre of the hill. Bait is placed inside the hollowed-out hill and a trap is set between the entrance and the bait. Small fur-bearing mammals are trapped this way (1977).

Top and above: Mary Rose, "Granny" Powder, harvesting blueberries at the age of ninety-three (Fort McMurray, 1978).

Right: High bush cranberries can be picked through the fall and winter, after the leaves have dropped and the berries have frozen on the vine. Bears, birds, and people all eat these berries. In the winter, a flock of birds will discover a grove of berries and wipe it out in a day or two. There are more than twenty edible fruit-bearing plants in the northern forest (Katy Sanderson, near Fort McMurray, 1977).

Top left and above: Bearberry. This plant produces a hard red berry which is eaten by animals and birds. The leaves ripen in the fall, turning red, then brownish. The image above is new green growth and the previous year's dried and brown leaves. Aboriginal traditional practice is to pick the fall leaf, dry it, grind it, and smoke it as traditional tobacco. The dried leaves may be mixed with other plants, such as red willow bark. Such mixtures also go by the name kinnickinnick.

Above: Bearberry leaves, ripened and ready to be crushed and used as kinnickinnick, a traditional tobacco. This plant grows in many environments, seeding itself in habitat ranging from wet bogs to rock covered ground. It grows low to the ground and often among blueberry and cranberry plants. Kinnickinnick may be picked in all seasons.

Pin cherry.

Strawberry.

Indian paintbrush.

Above and opposite page: Cotton is common to the bushlands and the High Arctic as well.

Above right and right: Sphagnum moss is a low, tufted, herbaceous plant that grows on rocks, at the foot of trees, and on damp soil. It is commonly found in the muskegs or peat bogs in the forest. In the fall, the moss dries and turns a rusty brown. The top of the plant is picked off and discarded, and the soft, light-brown layer of growth beneath is hung in the sun and breeze to dry. Once dried, moss can be used in a variety of ways: as an absorbent for baby diapers, as sanitary absorbent by menstruating women, as stuffing for pillows and bedding, and as stuffing to expand and clean containers made from bird or animal parts. It can be a dish cloth or chinking in log buildings. Many Aboriginal people traditionally used this natural product.

Far left: The bark has been stripped from the trunk of this tree. This is often done to allow the tree to dry in a standing position, which reduces warping and twisting in the grain of the wood. The stripped tree will be exposed to the sun and wind for a year, then cut off at ground level. Straight-grain wood is essential when making snowshoes, paddles, or toboggan runners. Sometimes, the bark is removed for use as shingles on a roof. In this case, when the tree is dry, it will be cut for firewood (Point Brule, Athabasca River, south of Fort Chipewyan, 1994).

Left: The lobstick tree sheds its lower limbs and develops a mass of cones and pine branches at the top. It is a travel guide if it is near a winter trail or near a shore visible to boat travellers. It is the traditional practice of Aboriginal travellers to give directions by this landmark (north shore of Great Slave Lake, 1956).

There are numerous types of lichens, actually symbiotic associations between algae and fungi. Lichens, among the hardiest of plants, are found on dead branches and rocks. They grow profusely in certain areas of the forest, and are a favoured food of caribou. Occasionally (when other foods are scarce), people eat the partially digested lichen found in the stomachs of the caribou they have killed. Caribou, like other deer and domestic cattle, have a chambered stomach which is capable of digesting cellulose, a component of raw lichen. People cannot digest this material and derive more nutritional benefit from eating the partially digested lichen than from directly consuming the plant itself.

Opposite page: This type of fence does not require fence posts to be sunk into the ground, as it is made of spruce poles, some of which are notched with an axe or saw to help hold them in place. This fence was built to enclose a yard (Conklin, 1993).

Right: The delta of Lake Athabasca is a habitat for waterfowl and aquatic mammals. This wandering stream provides access to the area for people in small watercraft.

Below right: Heavy rains have caused this stream in a heavily forested area to overflow.

Both of these places harbour mammals and waterfowl that have sustained a traditional way of life for centuries.

Above: Calling Lake.

Right: Athabasca River, approximately fifty miles north of Fort McKay.

Opposite page: Help prevent forest fires (Mile 12, Athabasca River, north of Fort McMurray, 1994).

HELP PREVENT FOREST

Wildlife

Until two hundred years ago, the people of the bushland sustained themselves solely on the natural resources provided by the forest. All animals, birds, and fish are edible, but some are favoured over others. The first criterion is availability; virtually any wild creature may be eaten in an emergency. However, if there is a choice of food, the second criterion is taste. Most people, for example, prefer the taste of whitefish over jackfish, and moose meat over beaver. Lean red meat is dried, fried, smoke-cured, or roasted. The tongue and heart are boiled and the heart and kidneys are roasted. Stomach fat and bone marrow may be eaten raw. Crackling, sometimes known as "Indian popcorn", is made from the stomach cape, and grease is saved from boiled bones and excess fat. Pemmican is made by drying and grating lean meat, then adding fat and berries.

Bear fat is stored in containers made from the bladder of a moose. The bladder is carefully removed from the carcass of the animal, then cleaned inside and out with water. Before it dries, it is stuffed with moss in order to stretch it to maximum capacity. When it has dried into shape, the moss is removed, and again the bladder is cleaned and warm bear fat is poured in. The fat solidifies as it cools, and the container is closed with a rawhide thong, or piece of sinew. If the fat is too hot when poured in, it will melt and shrink the bladder.

Tallow, as rendered fat is called, is usually made in the fall. It is left inside the moose bladder until it cools, causing it to solidify and turn white. It is then removed from the bladder with a bone knife or a sharp stick. If stored in a warm place, the tallow softens and can be spooned out. Additional heat will melt it back into a clear liquid that can be used for cooking.

ADDITIONAL PRODUCTS FROM MOOSE AND CARIBOU

Moose Antler Knife Handles

Antlers can be made pliable by boiling them. They are carved and shaped by cutting or rasping.

Water Bag and Fat Storage

The flesh, fat, and hair are removed from a piece of moose or caribou hide, which is then washed. The hide is stretched and shaped over a framework of sticks into a suitable bucket shape. It is stuffed with moss to absorb moisture and help it hold its shape. After the sticks and mass are removed, the rawhide will dry stiff and retain its shape. Finally, a rawhide handle is attached. This leather bucket will hold its shape when filled with cool water, but if filled with hot water, or allowed to warm in the sun, it may lose its shape (Isabel Ahyasou and many others, Fort McKay, 1994).

Katy Sanderson of Fort McMurray remembers her mother, Mary Rose Powder, using a moose bladder to store tallow at House River in the early 1920s, when this practice was common. Moose bladders are still occasionally used to store bear fat; James Grandjambe, Patsy Boucher, Annie L'Hommecourt, and many others have described this practice. A moose bladder prepared in the manner described will also function as a water bucket. The stomach or gut of a bear is also sometimes used to store fat (Maryanne [Boucher] Beaver, Fort McKay, 1994).

Blankets and Mattresses

Blankets, mattresses, pillows, and rugs are made from moose hide, often with the hair left on.

There are two species of caribou: the woodland caribou and the caribou of the Barren Lands. Woodland caribou are the larger of the two. A subspecies of the woodland is the mountain caribou found along the northern foothills of the Rocky Mountains. Woodland and mountain caribou are relatively rare and are found in isolated groups. While they do not migrate, their small herds do wander over large areas. The caribou of the Barren Lands live in huge herds, and as their name implies, spend most of the year in the High Arctic, where there are no trees. These herds migrate south to the fringes of the bushland in mid-winter.

Depending on where they live in the bushland, traditional hunters mainly rely either on moose, caribou, or on a combination of the two. The barren land caribou is smaller, yielding only fifty kilograms (twenty-three pounds) of meat per animal. A family of six people with ten dogs might require as many as one hundred fifty caribou per year if they relied on them as a primary food source. Of course, a plentiful supply of alternative foods, such as fish or commercial foods from the south, could reduce the need to harvest caribou.

Catching and preserving meat and fish serves to replenish the food supply, of course, but it also cements social bonds among family and friends. Spring hunting and fishing camps are places where people can visit, relieving the lonesome winter of trapping, and nights spent in distant line cabins.

Cured dried meat is a gift for special friends, especially Elders who are no longer physically capable of hunting and curing their own. In each community, there are some people who are exceptionally skilled at preparing such foods, and they are greatly respected for it. They take pride in sharing what they make.

Other big game animals are occasionally significant. Wood buffalo, elk, white-tail, and mule deer are all hunted when the opportunity arises. Grizzly and black bears are also hunted, particularly in the spring.

DRY MEAT

Meat is sliced into long strips about one centimetre thick. It is placed on a drying rack above a smoldering fire, where it slowly dries from the heat of the sun and the fire, and is cured by the smoke (Isabel Ahyasou, Fort McKay, 1994).

MEDICINE FROM THE MOOSE

Some Elders may recall stories of ancestors cooking and eating rumen, undigested food from the stomach of the moose. This has not been practised recently, but the rumen is still occasionally used as wound dressing. Gabe Orr of Fort McMurray remembered this, and applied rumen to a wound he received while using an axe to cut the ribs off a moose carcass. The rumen is said to help stop bleeding.

Around the uterus of the female moose, there are several nodules the size of marbles. These can be removed from the carcass, and pressed to the eyes to relieve the pain of snow blindness (Mary Tourangeau, Zachary Powder, and many others, Fort McKay).

BUSHLAND PRODUCTS – MOOSE

Approximately three hundred years ago, prior to the introduction of commercial products in western Canada, Aboriginal people relied fully on the resources of the land to sustain living and to develop a lifestyle that included cultural art as a mainstay of their being. All mammals, birds, fish, and vegetation played a part in that process. Aboriginal people fed, clothed, sheltered, and entertained themselves from the products of the land. They maintained a utilitarian and a spiritual relationship with the land. It is through this culture that we can come to understand the inherent value in the human being's connection with all creation. The moose and caribou, singled out to illustrate the subject of production, are among these creatures. Many of these are illustrated throughout the story and photo images of this book.

ART	ANIMAL SOURCE
clothing accessories	hair, hide, bone
carvings and painted images	antler
drawing and tracing images	tanned hide
necklace, or toggles	teeth, horn, bone
storytelling images	tanned hide
dream maps	tanned hide
fancy work of crafts (tufting)	hair
CRAFTS	
bow strings	rawhide
baby rattles	hide, sinew
drum covers	hide, sinew
ties and necklaces	hide, sinew, hair
TOOLS	
sewing needle and awl	bone
arrow	bone antler
bone knife	rib
hide scraper	leg bone

TOOLS *continued*

tent spike	rib, leg bone
handles for knives, saws	antler, bone
awls	antler, bone
eating utensils	antler, bone

CLOTHING

buttons	antler
thread for sewing	sinew
outer winter wear	hide with hair on
laces, rope	tanned hide
footwear	tanned hide
mitts, jackets, dresses, pants	tanned hide

HOUSEHOLD FURNISHINGS

mattress or pillow stuffing	hair
hat or clothing rack	antler
bedding, ground cover	hide with hair
travel blankets	hide with hair

HOUSING

frame covers	raw or tanned hide
chinking of logs	hair with mud
door hinges	raw or tanned hide
chinking of fireplace	hair with mud

EQUIPMENT

toboggan (carry all) wrap	hide
bags, storage	hide, stomach
moose call tree-scraper	shoulder blade
dog back pack	hide
dog harness	raw or tanned hide
dog collar	hide with hair
human back pack	hide, lower leg
snowshoe webbing	rawhide
snowshoe, foot binding	tanned hide

MISCELLANEOUS

gun case	tanned hide
knife sheath	tanned hide
luggage, bags, and purses	tanned hide
tanning chemicals	brain, urine
dog bedding	hair
eye sun shields	nodules of womb
soap	fat
storage bag for fat	bladder, stomach
straps, rope, laces, and thongs	tanned hide, raw hide
knife handles	antlers

FOOD GIFTS AND DELICACIES

Certain parts harvested from animals, including the nose, tongue, heart, and liver, may be bestowed upon members of the community who are deserving of the affection of the hunter. These include Elders, medicine people, midwives, and people suffering from illness. These parts hold special cultural and social significance, and sharing them is seen as a social grace.

With little other food resources, a hunting family and their dog team will consume one hundred and fifty caribou of the Barren Lands per year, supplemented by fish. The source of this information is members of four Inuit families camped on the ice of Contwoyto Lake in 1957 and 1958. People on a diet high in moose or caribou must eat eyes, brain, marrow, and fat and lean meat to obtain the nutrients necessary for human survival. Caribou eat lichen and moss. In its original state, this vegetation cannot be digested by humans, but after being processed to the stage of rumen in the first stomach of a caribou, it can be digested by humans and is a source of green food. All parts of the animal are good food. This reference comes from a caribou hunt by Fort Rae Dogrib First Nation people, which took place in January 1956.

Previous page:
These hunters were taking part in a two-night caribou hunt that took place in minus thirty-seven degrees Celsius (thirty-six degrees Farenheit) weather. The hunters spent the night outdoors and slept without tents in down-filled bags and blankets laid over snow, spruce boughs, and caribou hides. The sun had set at 4 p.m.; moon and stars shone brightly overhead. The only shelter prepared was a windbreak of small spruce trees, cut and placed at the hunters' backs. A fire provided warmth to dry the clothing, and as one side of their clothing dried, the men would turn to dry the other. It is important, at such cold temperatures, to prevent clothing from being dampened by perspiration, which can later freeze. Each man wore just enough for comfort, and stored extra clothing to keep it dry. While drying out and warming themselves, the men cooked various parts of the caribou they had killed. A hindquarter was propped against a log where it cooked slowly, and the nose and tongue were boiled in a pail of water.
The man with the pipe is Joe Beaulieu. He placed the head of the caribou in the fire to burn off the hair. Removing the head from the fire, he scraped off the remainder of the hair with his hunting knife. At the same time, he punctured each eye. Having done this, he placed the head back on the fire to cook it through. When the cooking was complete, he took the head from the fire and, bite by bite, consumed every bit of it, including the brain and eyes. He similarly prepared a leg of caribou. After removing the meat, he split the bone and consumed the marrow.

This is an example of eating all parts of the animal in order to achieve a more nutritionally-balanced diet. Lean meat alone, of which there was plenty, will not sustain good health over a long period. Fifty-five hunters, two hundred fifty dogs, 25,000 caribou, and the author of this book (who observed and carefully followed the advice and routine of the hunters) were all present at this event.

Opposite page: The moose is the largest member of the deer family. It is found throughout the bushland. Because of its large size, a moose represents a tremendous source of food, as well as raw material for dozens of traditional craft items, from clothing to tools. Virtually no part of the moose goes unused.

Julian Nanemahoo illustrates the use of a birchbark bugle to call a male moose. During the fall mating season, a bull moose will respond to a hunter who is able to imitate either the calls of a female moose or of another male. Skilled callers will imitate both calls. Confused, jealous, and enraged, a bull moose will often throw caution to the wind and approach to within a few metres of the hunter, looking for a bull rival to fight or a potential female mate. This is an effective tactic, though hunters, if their weapon is not at their side, risk being attacked by surprised bulls (Gods Lake, 1995).

Above: Tripe is the stomach tissue of a ruminant – in this case, a moose. Once cleaned, tripe may be eaten raw or cooked. Its folded shape, somewhat like the pages of a book, gave it its nickname, "the Bible".

This moose antler is deformed. It has many nodules, which are explained by Gordon Cardinal on the left. He hunted this unusual moose, which he believes barely escaped a wolf attack. A wolf, as wolves on the hunt will do, most likely approached the moose from behind and bit and hung on to the testicles of the moose. The moose escaped (likely due to the depth of the snow, which gave it a chance to outrun the wolf), but was castrated, no longer to be a real bull. He lived through the ordeal only to be captured a year later by Gordon. The loss of testicles causes a hormone imbalance which results in the deformed growth of the antlers. Gordon's older brother, François, a seasoned hunter, says that moose will rarely survive a wolf attack after having lost their testicles.

Above: Caribou hunt, southeast of Yellowknife. Joe Beaulieu is dressing out a caribou of the Barren Lands. The head, internal organs, and legs just below the knee joint are removed. The hide is left on to protect the meat against external contamination while in transit and while in storage (January, 1956).

Opposite page: Archie Cardinal is pictured removing a northern pike (jackfish) from a net (Mile 156, Athabasca River, south of Fort Chipewyan, 1978).

FISH

Fish is an important source of food for people in the bushland. Of all the game resources, fish are the most reliable, with predictable migrations year after year. The preferred species vary from place to place, although lake trout and walleye, also known as pickerel, are always favoured. Curiously, the northern pike, or jackfish, is not thought to be good to eat, even though it is considered desirable in other cultures. Pike are often used to feed dogs, or as bait to trap mammals.

In the old days, fishing took place mainly during fish migrations, as they moved up streams to spawn in the spring or fall. Before Europeans introduced nets and steel fish hooks, most fish were caught in fish traps, which were simply stone or log dams that channeled a spawning stream into a constricted area. Fish were speared as they swam upstream but would simply swim through the trap if it was left unattended. A beaver dam was often a convenient starting point for the construction of a trap. In the winter, fish were sometimes lured to within spearing distance of a hole in the ice with bone or antler lures. Bone jigs were also used, in a technique very similar to that used by modern ice-fishers for sport.

Nowadays, most Aboriginal fishing is done with gill nets. These nets have a mesh large enough to allow immature fish to swim right through them. Fish of the desired size are caught when the mesh allows the fish to get its head and fins through, but will not allow the fish's entire body to pass. Gill nets are used to catch migrating fish in rivers, and year round in lakes. Although it is more awkward to use gill nets once the lakes are frozen, it is still possible to string them in one hole in the ice and out another, so that the net hangs between the two holes like a curtain into the water below the ice.

Fish are consumed in many ways: fresh or frozen fish may be boiled or fried, while cured fish are eaten as is, boiled, or baked. Fresh fish are commonly grilled over an open fire, on a rack made of green willow which is resistant to burning.

To prepare a fish for cooking over an open fire, the fisher slits it along the belly, from gills to tail, removing the head and entrails. Two sticks are pierced through the thick part of the flesh to hold the fish flat. The pierced fish is then placed on a forked stick, which holds the fish, skin side up, just above the flames.

Generally, fish are either frozen, cured, or eaten fresh shortly after they are caught. In warm weather, a fish is cured within hours in order to minimize rot, but, in the winter, fish can generally be frozen right where they are caught simply by leaving them out on the ice. Modern bush people who have access to electricity may have their own freezers. Large community freezers have also been established in some towns. Through the winter, while the temperature remains below freezing, fish can be stored where they will be safe from scavengers, such as ravens. In the spring, when temperatures rise above freezing, such stockpiles will be thawed and then cured.

Fish is cured by exposure to heat, smoke, and dry air. Fish cured rare are not fully dried and must be cooked within a few days of curing in order to be safe to eat. Fully dried fish do not need any additional cooking, and will keep for several weeks. In addition, the lack of moisture makes dried fish lighter and easier to transport.

To prepare fish for curing, the fisher removes the head, fins, and entrails. Sometimes the skeleton is also removed, leaving a pair of fillets linked along the back. The fish is opened out flat, and a series of cuts are made, penetrating half the depth of the meat. These cuts expose as much of the fish as possible to the heat, smoke, and dry air.

Fish are sometimes cured in the open, above a smoky, smouldering fire, in which case the sun and breeze help to dry out the flesh. However, it is more common to cure fish in a conical tent, similar to a teepee, usually found at a base camp, or in a regular spring fish camp. Inside the tent, the fish is hung over willow racks. A small fire in a pit in the floor burns just enough to warm the air in the tent and surround the fish with smoke. The fish absorb the flavours of the smoke, and different wood, roots, or bark create different tastes. Dry-rot willow root is a favourite of the bush people. This curing process takes from three to five days.

Fish destined for use as dog food are often hung to dry whole. This method of preservation is usually used in cold weather. The fish are hung head down on skewers and placed on racks to allow air to circulate around the carcasses. The racks are high enough to be out of dogs' reach. A dead raven is sometimes used as a scarecrow to reduce scavenging by birds. At feeding time, a dry fish is taken from the rack and tossed to each dog.

In the winter, netting fish is fraught with hazards. The weather is cold, and there is no protection from the wind out on a frozen lake or river. If the ice is not thick enough – ten centimetres (four inches) being the minimum thickness for safety – there is the added risk of getting wet, which is extremely dangerous under such conditions.

The ice can also be too thick, up to two metres (seven feet), in which case it is very difficult to make a hole through the ice to the water. After the hole is made and the net is set, there is the risk that the net may be frozen to the underside of the ice or that several centimetres of ice will freeze the net into the hole, making it difficult to pull the net without damaging it or losing the fish.

The gill nets used are about ten metres (thirty-three feet) long and two metres (seven feet) deep, with a ten-centimetre (four-inch) mesh. Small fish, under a kilogram (two pounds), will swim right through the net, while larger fish are caught.

To set the net, two twenty-five centimetre (ten-inch) holes are made, about ten metres apart in the ice. Ropes are attached to the top corners of the net. A series of several floats are attached across the top of the net, and weights are attached along the bottom. One of the top corner ropes is attached to a float, called a jigger, which is pushed into one hole and manoeuvred past the other hole, where it is pulled up. Using the attached rope, the net is pulled down the first hole and along the underside of the ice to the second hole.

The net hangs down into the water, suspended between the two holes. In shallow water, poles may be driven into the bottom to hold the net in place. These poles must not be cut from fresh, live wood, as beavers remain active under the ice and will take the poles for food. The net is checked every day, as the best meat comes from fish taken alive from the net. Dead fish left in the net will decay, even in very cold water.

Willy Grandjambe stands along the shore at Moose Lake, at the location of a fish trap used in the 1920s. The stones which formed the trap are still visible from the shoreline (Birch Mountain region, 1994).

Dogrib hunters and trappers gather after spending the winter in their isolated camps. Here they visit friends and relatives, attend to general maintenance chores, and fish until it is once again time to head back to their traplines (Fort Rae, Northwest Territories, Spring 1955).

Joe Punch is netting fish beneath the ice (top) and grasping a rope attached to the exit end of a fish net (above). Note the rope in the upper right corner which is attached to the entry end of the net (Joe Punch, Samba K'e [Trout Lake], 1994).

A pole driven into the bottom helps to hold a fishing net in place (Joe Punch, Samba K'e [Trout Lake], 1994).

Top: This jig is used to help set the net below the ice (Joe Punch, Samba K'e [Trout Lake], 1994).

Above: The fish from this net are lake trout, fresh water cod (burbot), and northern pike (jackfish) (Trout Lake, November 1994).

Sony Football, Nigola Bruno, Isadore Charlo, Michel Cholka, Suise Bruno, John McKenzie, and Joe Beaulieu. These men from Fort Rae have travelled about sixty-five kilometres south to this spot, on the shore of Great Slave. The ice is still about one metre thick. Working together, the men set nets beneath the ice. The haul from a single net is visible in the foreground, while the accumulated catch of many days is visible piled up in the back.

This stockpile of frozen fish is set on an elevated stage where it can't be reached by small scavengers. When the fishing is done, it will be hauled back to Fort Rae, where this mountain of fish will be stored in a community freezer (a reefer) and distributed as needed to all members of the community (April 1956, Great Slave Lake).

FUR

It was the development of the Fur Trade which first brought European culture into contact with the bushland people. Beaver pelts were the most sought-after item to fur traders, and the trapping and sale of beaver pelts, as well as those of other fur-bearing animals, remains a significant source of cash for many modern bush people.

The beaver is only one of many fur-bearing animals that are trapped for their pelts. Because of its historical significance, most of this chapter is devoted to the beaver, although the bushland trapper knows each species well enough to fill an entire book on trapping lore.

ABOUT BEAVERS

Beavers are large rodents which eat the inner bark, small branches, and new growth of trees. Poplar trees are the beaver's main food, but a beaver will also eat alder, birch, and other vegetation. In order to reach the tender new growth high in trees, beavers will chew the tree down by gnawing at the trunk.

Beavers live in lodges made of mud and sticks. These dome-shaped structures are hollow, and may range in size from two to eight metres (six-and-a-half to twenty-six feet). Beaver lodges are located along river banks or in shallow water. The largest lodges are home to as many as four generations of beavers at the same time. When lodges become too crowded, younger generations will head out to build a lodge of their own.

Beavers are excellent swimmers, and they dive underwater to reach the entrance to the lodge. The living area of the lodge is dark but dry, located above water level.

Beavers are never far from water. In order to expand their feeding territory, and to move safely underwater, they build elaborate dams, raising water levels and flooding the forest. They also dig networks of ditches to reach fresh trees deeper in the forest. Beavers are active beneath the ice during the winter and will occasionally make breathing holes along travel routes to and from their lodges. Before the arrival of winter, beavers will cut and store hundreds of branches, which will be eaten beneath the ice. Many people believe that beavers gather far more food than they actually need; once the branches have dried, they will not eat them. Cutting down trees, building dams, flooding forests, digging ditches, and cutting and storing huge quantities of vegetation make the beaver quite unique: no animal, except man, has such a pronounced impact on the ecology of the boreal forest.

If the beavers eat all the new growth available near a lodge, they will abandon it in the spring and set off in search of a new territory, where the building process begins again. Otherwise, they rarely range far from their home, sticking to familiar waterways and feeder streams.

In order to mark their territory, beavers spray castorium, a musk which is secreted from two large glands, called castors, located at the base of their broad, flat tail. Beavers also have a pair of oil sacs which are attached to the castors. Both oil sacs and castors are used for medicine and perfume.

The quality of beaver fur is at its best in the winter season, when the coat has grown thick to protect the animal against cold. In the spring, beavers are caught at or below water level, and in the winter they are caught beneath the ice, in traps set near the entrances of their lodges.

Besides the fur itself, beavers are used in other ways. Beavers can be eaten, usually cooked whole over an open fire. The castor glands are removed and sold to perfume manufacturers around the world. The castor glands are also used to make a variety of medicines. For headaches, a piece of castor is gently heated until smoke permeates the room. Breathing the smoke relieves the headache. Smoke from a dried, powdered castor which has been sprinkled on burning wood is said to relieve a sore throat or nasal congestion. Powdered castor mixed with grease is applied to human wounds to reduce infection. A gummy secretion from the base of the gland can be chewed to relieve a sore mouth. Some bush people chew this gum simply for relaxation. Most hunters and trappers are also familiar with the practice of using a small piece of castor to lure predators like lynx into a trap. Many predators are willing to take a beaver caught away from the water, for on land the beaver is an ungainly, lumbering creature. It is as graceful underwater, however, as it is awkward on land; in this element it has little to fear from predators. Otters will occasionally destroy a beaver dam in order to catch a beaver kit, but will retreat if threatened by an adult.

A unique craft use of the beaver involved stuffing a beaver foot with fabric, hair, or wild cotton to use as a pincushion (Susanna, "Granny" Woodward, of Anzac, 1967).

CATCHING MUSKRATS

Muskrats can be caught as they escape from their dens, called push-ups. A person can approach the muskrat's den either by canoe, or by walking on the ice in the early spring. A net made with moosehide rope is laid over the exit of the den, which the bush people call the rat drain. When the person bangs on the push-up with a stick, the frightened muskrat runs out into the net, or is clubbed by the waiting hunter. Muskrat fur is cured and used to make jackets, mitts, and hats. It is also used to trim clothing and crafts. Muskrat, known simply as rat, is usually prepared by skinning, gutting, and cleaning the entire animal, and roasting it on a stick over an open fire.

MISCELLANEOUS GAME

Porcupine meat is light coloured, and has a texture similar to that of the domestic chicken. In order to make it safe to handle, the whole porcupine carcass is first placed in a fire to burn off the quills. The burnt hair and skin are then removed along with the internal organs. Porcupine is prepared by boiling, frying, or roasting.

Bear hides are used as rugs, mattresses, and blankets during winter travel. Bear meat is eaten by many people, and bear fat, which can be rendered into a clear oil, is used for cooking. Deer and fish oils are also used for cooking. The fat of animals, fish, or birds is mixed with ground dried meat and fruit to make pemmican, which is a traditional staple food of the region.

Only in an extreme emergency are wolves, coyotes, foxes, or dogs eaten. Generally, the animals which eat plants (the herbivores) are preferred to the animals which eat other animals (the carnivores).

Occasionally, religious beliefs influence food choices. The Dogrib people, for example, will not touch bear fat, nor will they ever kill a wolf, which is a sacred animal in their culture. This favour is returned to them, as there are no records of wolves killing Dogrib people.

Wolf hair is particularly long. It is often cut into strips for use as trim, especially around the hood of a winter parka. Wolf hide smells; wolves are said to urinate on each other, so the animals are always skinned outdoors, and hides are not taken indoors until they have been cleaned.

A BLANKET MADE OF THREE HUNDRED RABBITS

Rabbit is a mainstay in the diet of the bushland people. They are easy to catch in all seasons, and can be particularly plentiful when their population cycles peak. Rabbits' flavour is similar to that of the domestic chicken, and provides a pleasant change from a steady diet of red meat.

Tanned rabbit hides, with the fur on, are used as material for blankets and jackets, lining for mitts, trim for clothing, and as decoration for crafts. To make a blanket or a jacket, the pelts are cut into narrow strips, which are braided, and then woven together into a larger piece of material. A blanket might require as many as three hundred pelts, but at a time of peak populations, it might take as little as two or three days to snare such a number. Fifty to one hundred snares at a time are set along rabbit trails, in tangled natural deadfalls. Snares are made with sinew, roots, stripped bark, or thongs.

MEDICINES FROM FOREST ANIMALS

The liquid from the scent glands of a skunk can be mixed with water and applied with a sponge or cloth to the gums to relieve toothache. Soaked in a cloth and heated, this same mixture can be applied to a sore chest. The mixture was even prescribed for itchy skin. Zachary Powder remembers his mother treating him with skunk juice in 1948, when he was eighteen years old. Others who remembered the use of this Medicine include "Granny" Powder, Katy Sanderson, Elizabeth Shott, Johnny Orr, and Ernie Lacorde. Skunk scent glands, and even the entire skunk hide, could be placed in a tree near a house to ward off illness in the family who lived there ("Granny" Powder, Fort McMurray, and Mrs. Shott, Fort McKay, 1960s).

A large beaver dam, perhaps four metres (thirteen feet) high (northern Alberta, 1994).

A beaver dam in the early stages of construction. Note that beavers have stripped some of the branches of bark for food (northern Alberta, 1976).

Beavers cut trees of all sizes. This tree is about fifteen centimetres (six inches) in diameter. After the tree falls, the branches are removed, and the trunk is chewed into pieces small enough for the beaver to use in the construction of a lodge or dam.

When ice begins to form on the water in the fall, beavers stockpile food which will be frozen in place. This is retrieved and eaten as needed through the winter.

Right: François Orr prepares a trap to catch a beaver, whose pelt may become a hat similar to the one he is wearing (Fort McKay, 1978).

Above: Removing a beaver from a hole in the ice. The hole is situated over the runway that leads from the lodge to an under-ice feeding area.

Katy Sanderson, on her trapline (Fort McMurray, 1976).

Top left and right: Beavers living along major waterways do not need to build dams to control water levels. Thirty kilometres (nineteen miles) south of Fort McKay on the Athabasca River, the shore is littered with beaver-cut trees, near a lodge built into the riverbank.

Above left: Beavers will often build dams to flood swamps, raising the water level enough to swim to food sources and hide from predators.

Above centre: A muskrat push-up. This muskrat den is made of mud, grasses, and reeds. The name push-up comes from the muskrat's habit of building its den under the ice, and pushing a black mound of mud up through a hole in the ice.

Above right: An extraordinarily large beaver lodge – the height of a two-storey house. A beaver lodge this size might house as many as four generations of a beaver family.

Opposite page: Katy Sanderson checks her traps for muskrat and beaver (near Fort McMurray, 1978).

Bill Woodward tells the story that this wolf was old and appeared to be weary as it walked slowly along the shore between his house and a lake. Bill says that this is the largest wolf he has seen; its tail to nose measurement is three metres (ten feet). A male wolf is known to weigh one hundred and eighty pounds (eighty-two kilograms), while a female wolf weighs about one hundred and thirty pounds (sixty kilograms). Most wolves are smaller and lighter on average. Bill and his friend Grant Golosky are each six feet tall (Anzac, 1994).

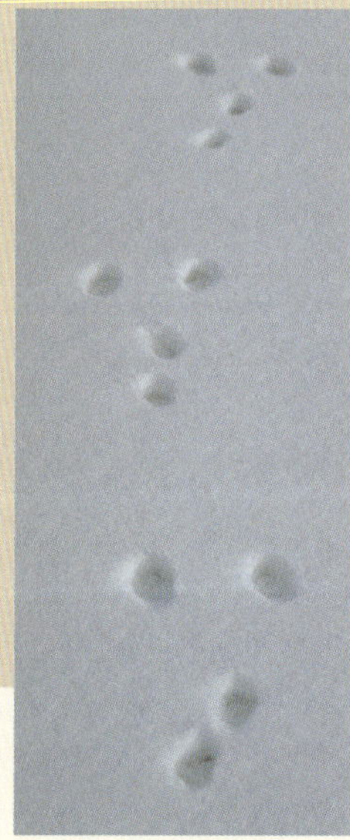

Hare (rabbit) tracks.

The Athabasca delta covers several hundred square kilometres at the west end of Lake Athabasca, in northeast Alberta. The delta and the shallows which extend up to four kilometres (two and a half miles) out into the lake are vital nesting habitat for millions of waterfowl, and the year-round home to a huge population of muskrat.

BIRDS

Migratory waterfowl are present from late spring until early fall. Ducks and geese, of which there are many species, are the favourite source of bird meat and eggs. Their fat is sometimes used for cooking, their down is prized as insulation, and feathers are used to decorate crafts. Three types of grouse live in the boreal forests year round and can be hunted and consumed. The ptarmigan, which migrates from the high arctic to the boreal forest during the winter, also makes for a nutritious meal. Owls and hawks are also occasionally eaten, but only if ducks and geese are not available. Occasionally, smaller wintering birds, such as buntings, are consumed.

MAKING A WATERPROOF BAG

Large waterfowl are still occasionally used to make rainproof skin bags. Loons were favoured for their attractiveness, though geese and pelicans were also used in earlier times. Neither loons nor pelicans are a common source of food, and in modern times it would be very rare for one of these birds to be killed to make a bag.

To make a birdskin bag, the skin was removed from the carcass, with the only incision being around the neck. Legs were removed at the first joint to eliminate a leg hole. The bag was packed with moss to stretch it and give it shape, and finished off with a collar of moose hide around the opening and a lace to draw it closed.

Such bags were used to store food, sewing notions, and virtually anything else small enough to fit within. They were often hung on walls as decoration or used as handbags. Zachary Powder's grandmother made such bags as recently as the 1940s, and birdskin bags were still used by James Grandjambe's family in the 1960s. Flora Grandjambe had one as late as 1995.

OTHER PRODUCTS FROM BIRDS

Waterfowl Down and Feathers Down refers to the fine feathers closest to the body of ducks and geese. After washing and drying, down can be used as particularly warm and lightweight insulation. Down and small feathers are used to fill pillows, quilts, and winter parkas.

Owl and Goose Wings These large wings are allowed to dry and are then used as brooms or dusters.

Owl Meat Roast owl tastes like domestic turkey.

Duck or Goose Meat Can be roasted, boiled, fried, or slowly turned on a green branch over an open fire.

Waterfowl and Shorebird Eggs Duck, goose, and seagull eggs are used in various recipes, or are simply hard-boiled to eat.

Bird wings, allowed to rot, are used as bait. The odour attracts small fur-bearing animals (Joe Punch, Samba K'e [Trout Lake], 1994).

Many birds are not regularly consumed by the bushland people. However, all birds and eggs are edible, and have been used as a food supply when other foods were not available.

The forest, from its floor and its shrubs to the limbs and highest peaks of its trees, is the meeting, breeding, incubation, and birth place of hundreds of species of the world's bird population. It is the nesting place for the rarest of birds, such as the whooping crane, and for thousands of migratory waterfowl, shorebirds, songbirds, hawks, eagles, or upland birds. It is the year-round home of snowbirds, ravens, whiskeyjacks, and four types of grouse. Birds without a forest are birds without a means to sustain their own species.

Above: Eagle nest. *Opposite page: Grey owl.*

The Canada Goose is a favourite source of meat, eggs, down, feathers, and whole skins for bags. The metal band on this bird's leg was placed there to help conservationists learn about the bird's movements and biology.

The pelican has an elastic pouch below its bill. This pouch was sometimes used by bush people to make a bag to carry small objects such as medicines (Isabel and William Ahyasou and many others, Fort McKay, 1994).

In the spring, great numbers of ducks arrive to nest in the boreal forest. They are a source of meat, eggs, down, and fat, and the feathers are used for decoration. They also serve as bait for traps.

Travel and the means to get around

On Foot

Checking sets on a trapline or stalking game is still often done on foot. When deep snow covers the ground, snowshoes are worn. When the need arose, bush people walked up to thirty kilometres (nineteen miles) per day for several days in a row; or up to a fifty kilometres (thirty-one miles) in a single trip, with only short rest breaks.

By Water

The canoe was invented by Aboriginal people to enable them to travel on the thousands of lakes and rivers that crisscross the boreal forest. These are the roads and highways of the bushlands. Although outboard motors have replaced paddling on many bushland journeys, canoes are still a vital means of transportation. No other boat design has enough cargo capacity to transport a moose carcass, yet remain light enough to be carried between lakes.

The shape of most canoes was similar, but they varied in size, from one-person rat canoes to large freight canoes. The so-called rat canoes are exceptionally small and manoeuvrable, designed for the shallow water, and are encountered when trapping muskrats and beavers. A rat canoe is about three metres (ten feet) long, one metre (three and one-third feet) wide, and thirty centimetres (twelve inches) deep. It is easily paddled or portaged by a single person. At the other extreme are freight canoes, which may reach ten metres (thirty-three feet) in length, and carry loads of several tons. A freight canoe would be paddled and portaged by two or more people. In modern times, all freighters are equipped with outboard motors. Touring canoes are typically five to seven metres in length, and carry loads of one to two tons. They are light enough to be dragged out of the water by one person, but would usually be portaged by two people.

The traditional birchbark canoe was one of the bushland culture's most elegant design achievements. This canoe was built on a frame of birch or spruce wood, which was bent into shape and tied with moosehide thong or rope made of spruce root.

Removing the birchbark from the tree required special seasonal timing and technical knowledge. The birchbark was patched together and laced to the frame with spruce rope, and sealed with spruce sap. It was often decorated with images of birds and

Jimmy Fish, well ahead of the dog teams, breaks trail (northeast of Fort Rae, 1956).

animals, drawn with an orange clay called ochre. Canoes were also built with hulls of moosehide, and more recently, out of canvas.

Paddles and oars were carved from jackpine or spruce. These woods were preferred because they contained a lot of resin, which serves as a natural preservative and water repellant.

Motors

In the last one-hundred years, motors have had a dramatic impact on water transportation in the bushlands. In earlier times, several paddlers were needed to keep a freight canoe on course if the wind was blowing against it. Today, large freight canoes and skiffs are all equipped with outboard motors, enabling them to be handled by one person. Equipped with motors, boats carry heavier loads at faster speeds, especially when travelling upstream. Trips of hundreds of kilometres are made easily, bypassing the old stopover camps.

The Chipewyan skiff has a square stern suitable for mounting an outboard motor. Typically handmade by a trapper, a skiff has a wooden hull made of boards which were either lapped one over the other, or butted together. The hull is caulked with a mixture of spruce gum or tar, and ochre.

On Snow

One of the enduring images of the northern forests is a team of dogs pulling a toboggan over a heavy blanket of snow. Toboggans, also called carryalls, were pulled by dogs, people, or even by a tame moose or caribou. In northern Europe, reindeer (European caribou) are still used for this purpose. Modern bush people still use carryalls, but they are more likely to be pulled by a snowmobile. Sled dogs are now mostly used for recreation and racing.

A typical carryall is about four metres (thirteen feet) long and half a metre (one-and-a-half feet) wide. Fabric sidewalls about half a metre high enclose the load. The front of the toboggan is smoothly curved to help it run over loose snow and obstacles, while the last half metre at the back is flat; it is here that the musher (driver) stands. On tight, twisting trails, the musher frequently has to leap off to lift and steer the back of the sled over or around obstacles. The load is secured with tanned or rawhide ropes, as the carryalls occasionally flip over during travel.

A builder keeps the terrain he needs to cover in mind while building his carryall. A larger toboggan will require more exhaustive trail-clearing, so if the terrain is particularly rough, a bush person will likely build a smaller, more manoeuvrable sled.

The load pulled by a dog team is typically about equal to the combined weight of the dogs and the person driving them, the musher. A team is usually five to seven dogs. A day's journey would not usually exceed fifty kilometres (thirty-one miles), but a well-conditioned team pulling a light carryall over a good trail could conceivably cover one hundred and fifty kilometres (ninety-three miles) in a single day. On a short trip, a dog can pull up to three times its own weight.

To make a carryall, the bush person first needs to find a tamarack or birch tree. With practice, it is possible to select a tree that will produce boards that are large enough, strong enough, and straight enough for the base of the toboggan. The normal practice is to choose several trees and strip them of their bark. These are left standing for a year to dry, after which they are cut. The essential dimensional boards are cut from the tree that is straightest after drying.

After the boards have been cut and planed, they are bent into the curve they will need to form the front of the carryall. The boards must first be soaked in hot water and then placed in a form constructed of poles to gain the desired shape. They are steamed for several days, and their curve is progressively tightened with the help of tightening moosehide thongs. Two boards are placed side-by-side and joined by a series of crossmembers. The carryall is tied together with rawhide lacing. A backboard, about sixty centimetres (twenty-three inches) high, is mounted at the rear of the cargo area.

A safety rope extends several metres past the back of the carryall, which is used by the musher to help steer the sled and to slow the sled when running down hills. Some builders also add a foot brake at the back of the sled. Another method of slowing the sled is to let a rope or chain slip over the front and then under the toboggan to act as a drag. If conditions are icy, or rocks are beginning to show on the trails in the spring, runners are added to the bottom of the carryall. The purpose of runners is to stop sideways slippage and reduce wear and tear on the base of the sled.

In deep, fresh snow, the bush person will often break trail for the dogs by walking ahead of them on snowshoes. The dogs repay such favours by using their superior senses and instincts to find the way home in darkness and blizzards. An experienced lead dog will sense where the musher is going, and find the way even on the featureless expanse of a frozen lake. Trappers often comment, "You're never stranded with a good dog team; they'll take you home day or night, in any weather."

Trail in the spring.

The hard-packed snow of a winter trail sinks into muskeg, leaving an indentation which lasts for years.

Left: Archie Burke in search of food in the form of upland birds or animals. Wet muskeg and low bush foliage is difficult to navigate with equipment in the summer season. Summer overland hunting is primarily on foot from river or lake shorelines (Fort Fitzgerald, 1980).

Top and above: Katy Sanderson checks her sets. A trail through the bush may be as narrow as the width of the shoulders of the hunter. The lead dog of the team pulling a toboggan may be out of sight of the driver on some of the sharp turns on trails such as this (Fort McMurray, 1977).

Above: Around 1960, snowmobiles began to replace dogs as the pullers of toboggans like this one. The black band is a portion of a car tire spliced in the towing rope to act as a shock absorber (Garden Creek, Wood Buffalo National Park, 1989).

Left: Detail of the rear of a toboggan, showing backboard, and crossmember laced to base boards, where the musher stands.

Above left: Detail of the front curve of a toboggan, shaped by soaking, steaming, and bending the boards. This replica is enclosed with rawhide.

Above: Dogs' superior senses and instincts are useful in poor weather, or on routes where landmarks are few and far between. A lead dog will faithfully lead the team on a trail (Jimmy Fish, Fort Rae, 1956).

Above and right: The first trip of the season after a heavy snowfall on trails like this will be packed by the dog musher on snowshoes. Pictured is a dog team pulling a loaded toboggan through a bush trail (northeast of Fort Rae, 1956).

Left: A midday lunch stop on a trip. The daylight hours extend rapidly during the spring season. Jimmy Fish has returned from a campfire location to his dog team. The author's team is resting in the snow. They too received lunch, a quarter of a pound (one-tenth of a kilogram) of tallow (lard) and a small portion of fish (northeast of Fort Rae, March 1956).

A modern-day dog-team trail crossing of a paved highway with an aircraft jet stream overhead (1996).

When skies are clear, the traveller and dogs can easily identify the contours of land and the trail that they are on by the light of the moon and stars reflected off the snow. On a clear night in midwinter, the time to stop is often known by the position of the big dipper. When the handle of the dipper points to the ground it is 10:30 p.m. in this region of northern Canada (Jimmy Fish, Fort Rae, 1956).

Since the 1950s, the snowmobile has become the principal vehicle for winter travel. Toboggans are still towed behind them when hauling cargo. Somewhat more recently, wheeled all-terrain vehicles have also become a common sight in the bushlands.

François Auger-Cardinal on a trail near his cabin on the shore of Orloff Lake, using an all-terrain vehicle (Calling Lake, 1995).

Above: Net fishing is a traditional practice among bushland people (Chipewyan Lake, 1995).

Opposite page: Chipewyan skiffs with outboard motors travel on the Athabasca River (near Poplar Point, 1964).

Top: A small stream thirty metres (ninety-eight feet) from Katy's trapline residence. A muskrat and beaver habitat, constructed by beaver (near Fort McMurray, 1976).

Above: Louie Martin pulling a net near his fishing camp, where dry-smoked meat is being prepared (Fort Chipewyan, July 1980).

Opposite page: A fall morning on the Athabasca River. Fog is common when cool air meets warm water, and it can often reduce vision to mere metres, making travel by boat impossible. The fog lifts and dissipates after the sun warms the air (Mile 42, Athabasca River, near Fort McKay).

Above: When caribou were scarce in their region the Dogrib people made a four-hundred kilometre trek northwest of Fort Rae to the Barren lands, travelling by canoe on a lake and river route joined by fifty-five portages. This lead canoe outfitted with an eight-horsepower outboard motor is pulling two other canoes. Together, the three canoes carry nineteen people and enough food supplies and hunting gear for a seven-week trip. To conserve fuel, passengers will paddle; the motor will be used only to cross a large body of water and to help upsteam on rivers (Russell Lake, near Fort Rae, 1955).

Above: Dogrib hunters shoulder heavy packs filled with clothing, bedding, tents, hunting gear, and food. They will carry all their gear and canoes on lake-to-lake portages and continue paddling (Russell Lake, near Fort Rae, 1955).

School bus (Janvier, 1976).

School bus. Drivers are John James Janvier and Jean Cardinal (Janvier, 1965).

A team of horses, hitched to a school bus, transports children to school. School bus transportation is a business in several communities in northern Alberta (Peerless Lake, 1989).

Art and crafts

For thousands of years, the plants and animals of the boreal forest provided everything for the bushland people: all of the tools and clothes which they needed for survival; the arts and crafts which brought enjoyment to their lives; and the spiritual objects with which they practiced their religion. Many of the artifacts once used in daily life have now been replaced by manufactured goods which are more efficient and convenient. In some cases, skills which were once common are now known by just a few Elders. Nowadays, some traditional crafts are practiced not for the sake of utility, but to preserve a fragile culture, so that it may be handed down to the next generation.

MOCCASINS AND MUKLUKS

Moccasins are the most common type of footwear among bush people. They are worn by all members of the family for all occasions, in both summer and winter. Footwear for everyday use is often plain, made of undecorated moose, deer, or caribou hide. The favoured material for the sole of the moccasin is the thick hide from a mature bull moose, though the hide is also the most difficult to tan and sew. On special occasions, elaborately-decorated moccasins are worn. They may feature leather fringes, fur trim, moose hair tufting, fish scale or porcupine quill beading, and embroidery of silk, cotton, or wool.

While the shape of men's and women's moccasins is similar, their decoration is different. Women's moccasins can be decorated with rabbit fur or the light, soft fur from the belly of a muskrat. The soles are often made of white deerhide. Beadwork usually takes the form of small floral patterns. Men's moccasins are decorated with beaver fur, or the dark, coarse fur from a muskrat's back. The soles of men's moccasins are tanned brown. While men's moccasins may also feature floral beadwork patterns, these tend to be larger and more subdued in colour than the patterns that appear on moccasins worn by women.

Mukluks are soft boots that extend up to just below the knee. The bottom of a mukluk is similar to a moccasin, while the upper portion is made of moosehide, cloth, canvas, or fur. A thong draws the top of the leg tight to keep the mukluk up. There is room inside for several layers of warm fabric. Wool socks, felt insoles, and liners of felt or fur jointly serve this purpose.

Opposite page: These mukluks worn by Margaret MacDonald were made by Victoria MacDonald. Whole families may have matching mukluks for special occasions (Fort McKay, 1995).

This page: Various moccasins.

Opposite page: Meleni Houle holding moosehide moccasins she made (Trout Lake, 1995).

Bottom row right: Adult mukluks: moosehide soles and stroud leggings, decorated with silk embroidery (Ms. Lafferty, Fort Rae, 1955).

Sweetgrass has a pleasant scent either fresh or dried. It can be hung in a room as an air freshener or used in the making of art and crafts. Sweetgrass smoulders when burned, and produces a smoke which symbolically purifies.In modern times, sweetgrass is part of spiritual and ceremonial gatherings, including mixed gatherings of Aboriginal and non-Aboriginal people. It is passed from person to person, or taken around to each person by a member of the group. The Sweetgrass Ceremony is common to many Aboriginal cultures.

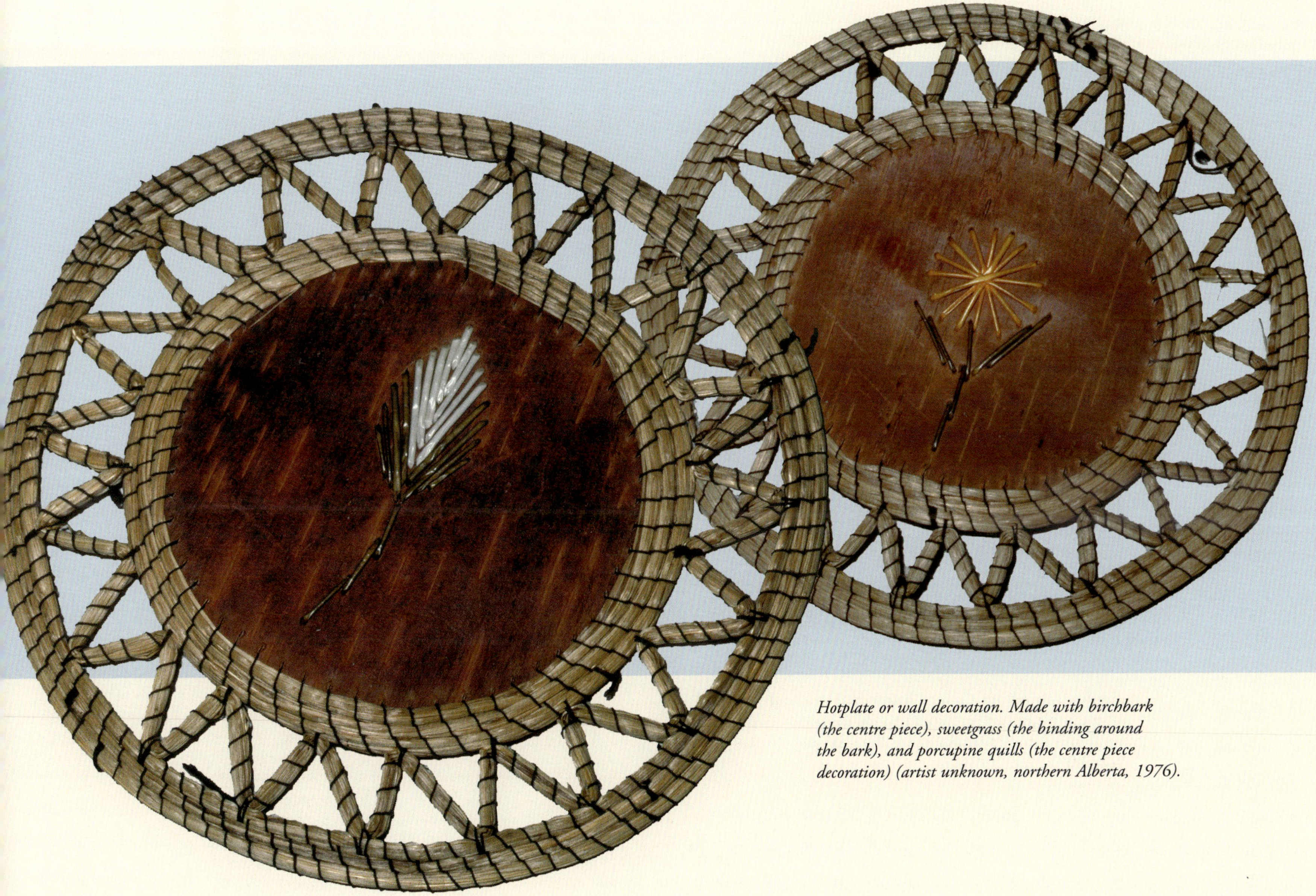

Hotplate or wall decoration. Made with birchbark (the centre piece), sweetgrass (the binding around the bark), and porcupine quills (the centre piece decoration) (artist unknown, northern Alberta, 1976).

Caribou hair tufting. Caribou hair is dyed the colours shown and each hair is stitched into the tanned moosehide backdrop for this design (Lucy Simon. Jean Marie River, 1994).

Carved moose antler
(Garry Cooper, Fort McKay, 1994).

There are many ways to use a moose antler – fashioning a pendant is one way.

Isabel Net is known to her family by her Aboriginal name, Nestawastanum (Trout Lake, 1995).

Isabel is scraping the hair off a moosehide, a laborious task among the many steps taken to produce fabric for clothing.

Alice Boucher holding a hide scraper made from the leg bone of a moose. This small tool is used to scrape the flesh from the hides of small animals (Fort McKay, 1994).

Artisans of Traditional Culture

Top: Melanie Bigstone at age eighty-two (Desmarais, 1995).

Above: Sophie Auger at age seventy-two (Desmarais, 1995).

Above: Mary McKenzie (Anzac, 1993).

Top: Margarite Beauregard at age seventy-eight (Desmarais, 1995).

Centre: Lucy Cardinal at age seventy-six (Desmarais, 1995).

Above: Nancy Woodward sewing beads onto tanned moosehide (Anzac, 1993).

Top: *A beaver hat provides excellent insulation on cold winter days.*

Above: Beaver fur mitts. The palms are moosehide and the lining is fur.

Flora Grandjambe, a skilled artisan whose work is shown on this and the following two pages (Fort McKay, 1994).

Left: A purse made from the spotted hide of a fawn. Fawn hides are used in crafts when a fawn is found dead, or found in the body of a dead female deer. Because of their beautiful markings, such hides are sought after for crafts (Fort McKay, 1994).

Below: Moosehide pouch with bead embroidery.

Above: Necklace made with claws of a black bear (Fort McKay, 1994).

Opposite page: This necklace was made by stringing the teeth of a black bear over a moosehide thong.

Katy Sanderson at age eighty-one (Fort McMurray, 1993).

Below: Traditional decoration applied to modern materials. This handbag, made by Katy Sanderson, consists of a velvet background decorated with commercial beads (Fort McMurray, 1963).

Tom Wanyandie (Wanyandie Flats, north of Grande Cache, February 1999).

Top right: Lucy Wanyandie at age eighty-two (Grande Cache, August 1999).

Above and right: This is a waist belt, approximately one metre (three-and-a-third feet) long, decorated with dyed porcupine quill on a background of black satin. It was made circa 1890 by a family member – possibly the grandmother – of Lucy Wanyandie of Grande Cache long before Lucy was born.

Fish hook. Willow wood shaft, bone point, sinew. Hooks such as these were attached to a willow branch pole or to a rope (moosehide thong, for example) (unknown artist, northern Alberta).

Top left: Fish net needle made of spruce wood. This tool is used to knit or crochet a fish net out of string. To make a fish net needle, one needs resin (sap) saturated fir, spruce or pine wood, and the skill of a person who can whittle (Alice Boucher, Fort McKay, 1994).

This type of knife sheath, which was held to the waist by a thong, was made of tanned hide decorated with plastic beads. Traditional embroidery made use of porcupine quills or animal hair, coloured with natural dye. Later, glass beads, introduced in the early days of the European fur trade industry, were used. Today, commercial plastic beads are in common use.

A bone knife made from the rib of a moose, caribou, or deer. This type of knife was used as a utensil to scrape hides, scale fish, or cut snow blocks. Maker unknown, but many Aboriginal traditional hunters and trappers know this skill.

Birchbark baskets are crafted in many styles and shapes. Traditionally, they were used to carry almost anything, including water. Such baskets are made of bark removed from the tree in the spring, when the bark is easiest to shape. The best birch trees are located near a river or lake, where the humidity makes the bark pliable. After removal from the tree, the bark is steamed and moulded into shape. Seams are sewn with spruce root and sealed with spruce gum. Leather thongs are used as carrying straps. The basket lid is hinged with moosehide thong (Elise and William McDonald, Fort McKay, 1965).

A natural design in which the inner surface of the birchbark is used on the outside of the basket to show off the natural pattern of the inner bark (Flora Grandjambe, Fort McKay, 1994).

Decorated birchbark basket. The lid is rimmed with sweetgrass, and the handle is made of a thin strip of wood.

Left: Packsack. The best hide for such packs is from the lower leg of a deer, moose, or caribou. The hair is short and the skin is tough and waterproof. The hide from several legs is needed to make such a bag. The top of the pack is rimmed with tanned moosehide, and includes a thong which pulls the bag closed. Such bags are equipped with shoulder straps, or a single strap for hand carrying (Mary and James Grandjambe [1966], Alice Boucher [1994], and many others).

Above: The skin and feathers of a loon. It serves as a waterproof and dustproof container for travel items that must remain dry, including moss, kinnickinnick, food items, and, since the European fur trade days, matches. The hide is removed from the carcass so that only the neck hole is open. This is no longer a common practice (James Grandjambe family, Fort McKay, 1966).

Right: A loon-skin bag, underside up, produced by Flora Grandjambe (Fort McKay, 1994).

Birchbark biting. The snowflake design is created by folding a thin piece of birchbark, and then biting in a pattern of tooth marks. This art form is practised mostly by women (artist unknown).

Above: A hide scraping tool made from the lower leg bone of a moose. The thong helps the user to apply scraping pressure. Most Aboriginal persons who prepared skins made use of this tool.

Top left and right: A hand-held scraper fashioned from the lid of a metal container is used to scrape flesh from the hide of a fur pelt (Willy Grandejambe, Namur Lake, 1994).

Above: Birch wood and moosehide snowshoe made by Michel Gladue (Fort McMurray, 1974).

Right: Michel Gladue, in his skiff (Fort McMurray, 1974).

DRUMS

Hand-held drums are important accessories in traditional bushland cultural activities. Drums are typically about one metre (three feet) in circumference and seven centimetres (three inches) deep. The base of the drum is open. The drum is played with a bare hand or beaten with a bone or willow stick.

A drum is made by stretching a moosehide cover over a hoop of birch or spruce. Sometimes drums are covered with the skin of an unborn moose, deer, or caribou. The hide is laced on to the wooden hoop with rawhide thongs. The tone of the drum is determined by the thickness of the cover, the size of the drum, and the tightness of the cover. The hide shrinks and tightens when heat is applied, usually by holding it over an open fire.

Rawhide thongs are also drawn tight across the base of the drum. The drummer holds the drum at the point where these thongs cross. (Elise and William MacDonald (1963); Katy Sanderson (1993); James Grandjambe (1994), the gentlemen that follow this page, and many others).

This page: Baptiste Janvier created the drum he is using in the photograph.

Opposite page: Alphonse Beaver of Sandy Lake was born in 1899. Seen here in 1995, he remained active in traditional crafts. He made the drum he holds in this picture.

PIONEER
PRO CHAIN SAWS

Above: Waterfowl decoys are used when hunting ducks or geese. Decoys are carved from a variety of woods, although light, porous woods like aspen are easier to carve than are hardwoods. Pictured is Baptiste Janvier with hand-carved decoy (Conklin, 1993).

Below: A moose shoulder bone is used to imitate the sound of a bull moose scraping its antlers against a tree during the mating season. The sound produced helps attract both females and jealous males. Hunters use this sound, and a variety of calls, to lure animals into traps or within rifle range (Fred MacDonald, Fort McKay, 1994).

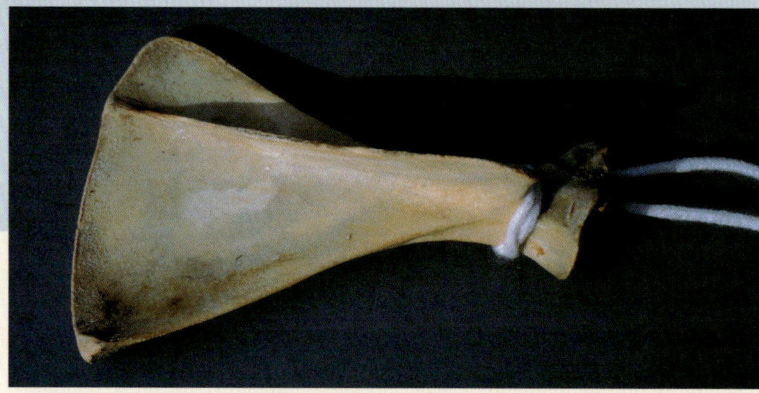

Above: This beaver shoulder bone is easier to carry than the larger deer or moose shoulder bone, but is still an effective way to gain the attention of a moose during a hunt.

Top: Spruce wood is naturally saturated with resin which helps to waterproof and prevent rotting of this paddle, hewn by a member of the Alice Boucher family (Fort McKay, 1994).

Above: Wood products are used to create the traditional canoe: birchbark for the hull, spruce wood for the frame, spruce root rope, and spruce gum for moisture proofing. This sixty centimetre (twenty-four inch) replica was made by Elise and William McDonald, an experienced traditional hunter couple (1966).

Left: A dugout canoe, two-and-one-half metres (eight feet) long, used in shallow water primarily to travel through muskrat habitat to harvest muskrat in the spring. This one is out of use in the yard of Virginia Rohatinsky at Wanyandie Flats (north of Grande Cache, 2000).

Far left and left: Fish scale necklaces. Scales are dried and coloured with berry juices and plant extracts. Each scale is separated by a piece of porcupine quill, a dried berry, or a bead. Glass beads and, later, plastic beads have replaced many natural materials in modern times.

Right: Birchbark baskets decorated with porcupine quills.

Left: A baby rattle. A strip of wood is curled upon itself, leaving one end to function as a handle. A tight covering of hide encloses a few stones.

Right: A grouse-gullet baby rattle. The gullet is a pouch in the bird's digestive system, located at the base of the throat. This one contains twigs, berries, bugs, and bits of soil eaten by the bird. After removal from the bird, the gullet is hung and allowed to dry and harden. The material within remains dry and loose. Tied off at the top, the dry gullet is used as a baby's rattle (Fred and Margaret MacDonald, Fort McKay, 1994).

Opposite page: The webbing (babiche) of a snowshoe is made of moosehide (cleaned of its hair, fat, and meat) soaked in tree resin.

Right: Snowshoes were regularly used by hunting or trapping bushland persons to attend to trapline sets located in areas not accessible by dog teams. This pair (child size) was made in 1963 by Elise and William McDonald (Fort McKay).

Sinew is tendon material that connects muscle to bone in living animals. Tendons, up to a metre (three feet) long and six centimetres (two-and-a-half inches) wide, are taken from neck and back of moose, deer, and caribou. After the tendon is dried, fibres are stripped off as they are needed. If a strong thread is needed, several fibres are rolled together. The dried threads are somewhat brittle. Before use, they are moistened with a small amount of water or saliva and allowed to soften.

Thongs, laces, and ropes are stripped from tanned hide in various lengths and widths. Such thongs are used for a multitude of purposes, from moccasin laces to snowshoe bindings and dog harnesses.

Rawhide laces. Rawhide is not as soft or flexible as tanned hide. It is used in the construction of such things as snowshoes, toboggans, or drums. When soaked in resin it is called babiche. *Traditional Aboriginal people produced this material from a variety of animal hides.*

Right: Rifle carrying case with shoulder strap, made of tanned moosehide (Katy and George Sanderson, Fort McMurray, 1967).

Far right: Top: Birchbark horn, used as a moose-call (Katy and George Sanderson, Fort McMurray, 1967).

Below: Salt shaker, made from a hollowed tree branch, with tanned moosehide cover.

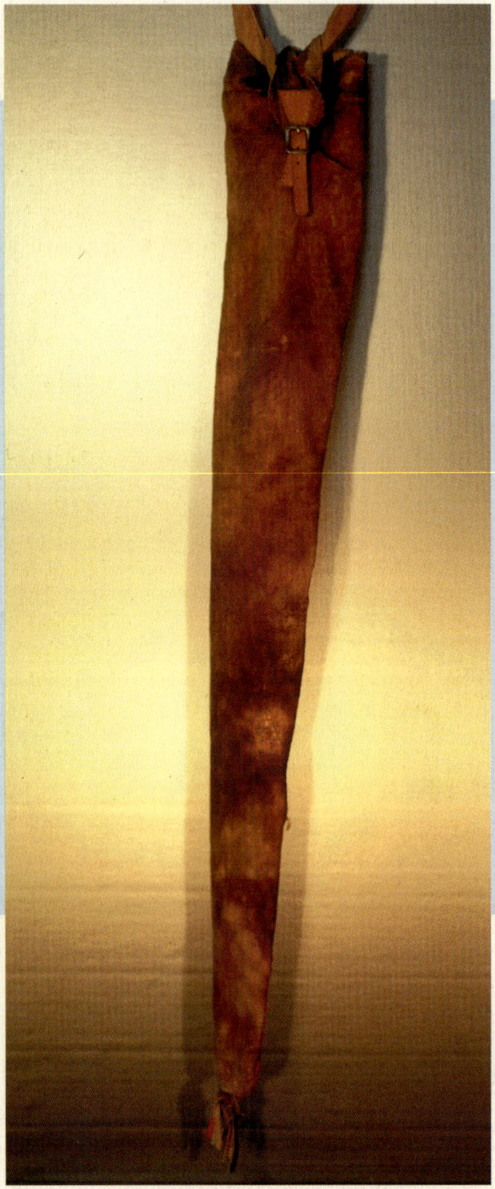

Above: Dog harnesses are made of moosehide. The collar is a moosehide tube filled with moose hair. It is custom sized and shaped to fit the neck and shoulders of each dog. The traces, back-strap, and stomach-cinch are also made of tanned or raw moosehide. Resin, an offensive-tasting substance, is applied to the harness to deter dogs from chewing the leather.

Opposite page: The tail of a ptarmigan, or (as illustrated) ruffed grouse is used as a fan, brush, or wall decoration. Its preparation is simple: remove it from the bird, fan it out, and let it dry.

Carvings set in the stump of a tree along the lake shore (Calling Lake, 1995).

Glossary of bushland language ~ English

Aboriginal: Being the first of its kind in a region; a first person. In Canada, Section 35 of the Constitution Act of 1982 defined Aboriginal peoples to include First Nations, Inuit, and Métis peoples.

antler: The deciduous horn of a member of the deer family, i.e., moose, caribou, elk, or deer. Often used by Aboriginal peoples in the production of art, crafts, and tools.

babiche: Rawhide (usually moosehide) soaked in resin (usually the sap of a spruce tree); it is commonly used as webbing in snowshoes.

backpack: A container, usually of fabric construction, carried on a person's back and used to carry supplies.

bait: Food, or an object that gives off the appearance, sound, or scent of food used to lure an animal, bird, or fish into a trap.

bannock: A heavy, flat, round bread made of flour, usually unleavened; a traditional recipe includes ground plant root and fish eggs.

barge: A flat, bottomed boat capable of carrying freight across rivers and lakes, and pushed or pulled by a motor boat. Sizes range from a load capacity of two tons to six-hundred tons or more.

barged: Goods and supplies carried or transported across a river or lake by a barge either pushed or pulled by a power boat.

bark: To remove the bark of a tree after it has been cut down; to bark a log or pole.

Barren Lands: Lands north of the boreal forest; a tract of land with inferior tree growth and little vegetation but rich in food for caribou and other mammals. It is a vast nesting habitat for many migrating birds.

birchbark: The protective cover of a birch tree. Used traditionally to cover a canoe frame and used extensively in the production of crafts.

birchbark imprint: The creative design made by tooth imprints bitten in a strip of birchbark; usually the practice of First Nations women.

black ice: Ice floe that is saturated with melt run-off; it may sink without warning.

boreal: Of, related to, or located in northern regions.

boreal forest: A large area of wooded land; a dense growth of trees and underbrush, relating to northern and mountainous parts of the northern hemisphere.

boughs: The fine branches of a coniferous tree; often refers to the small branches of a spruce tree, as in spruce boughs.

bow: The front end of a canoe or boat.

break-up: A time or season of year, especially early spring; the movement and breaking of ice across lakes and rivers in the spring as caused by melting.

break trail: To pack snow, usually with snowshoes, to allow access for walking or for dog team travel.

brush: The low growth of shrubs and grass; often mixed with tree growth; a forest ground cover.

bush person: A person occupying forest land; living in part or in total from the land.

cabin: A small house located along a trapline used by trappers as a temporary residence or overnight shelter; usually built of logs and consisting of a single room.

cache: A place for the storage of food and supplies; often located at strategic locations along the trapline and hunting route.

camp: A residence, home, and property in the northern bushland.

candlestick: Lake or river ice which, in the spring, is near break-up condition. Not safe to travel over.

carriole, carryall: A toboggan about four metres (thirteen feet) long and half a metre (one-and-one-half feet) wide, fitted with a fabric (moosehide) sidewall cover; used to carry people and supplies; pulled by dogs, snowmobiles, or all-terrain wheeled vehicles.

castors: Large glands located under the belly skin of both male and female beavers, by which the scent of the beaver is carried and dispersed. Castors are a source of traditional medicine and a market commodity for the contemporary commercial perfume industry.

castorium: Scent from the castor of a beaver; used in a variety of traditional medicines and to produce commercial perfume.

caulk: The act of filling seams or joints of boats and log buildings.

caulking compound: Material used to fill and seal the seams of boats and houses.

channel: A river or lake pathway for boats, especially relevant where there is a narrow channel meandering under the surface of a large body of shallow water.

chink: (see caulking) To fill the gap between the logs of a house; to fill the gaps between boards on a Chipewyan skiff to keep out water or air.

clearing: An area of land in a forest where trees are cleared out; similar area, cleared of trees, on the shoreline of a stream, river, or lake.

conical tent: (see teepee) A shape resembling a cone; the shape of an Aboriginal teepee.

crackling: Also known as Indian Popcorn, a sweet and crunchy snack made when the stomach cape of a moose is rendered to remove fat and then dried.

culture: Customary beliefs, values, and material traits of a racial or social group; the Aboriginal lifestyle.

deadwood: Fallen trees, often used as a refuge by animals and birds; source of dry firewood.

dog-musher: A person who controls and drives a dog team while it pulls a toboggan.

down: The next-to-the-body layer of feathers of a goose or duck; used for stuffing pillows, quilts, and clothing, and as lining in bird nests. The eider duck (female) is a preferred source of down.

downstream: In the direction of the flow of a river.

downwind: In the direction towards which the wind is blowing; to be downwind from the location of a hunted animal.

dressing an animal: Preparing the carcass of a hunted animal, bird, or fish; removing hide (skin), some bones, and entrails.

dry cure: A process of curing food, particularly meat and fish, in the open air over a trickle of smoke and heat from a wood fire.

dugout: (as in dugout canoe) This is a hollowed-out log fashioned to be a water transportation vehicle. A canoe is as short as two metres (six-and-one-half feet) and as long as the tree size will allow, usually ten metres (thirty-three feet) or more.

eddy: A place along a riverbank where the flowing water reverses its direction creating a circular flow of water; often still water bordered by a shore and a flowing stream; preferred place for travellers to rest or to place a permanent dock.

fishstick: About ten kilograms (twenty-two pounds) worth of fish hung head-down on a willow branch which has been pierced through the tail of each fish; a stick across which ten or twelve fish have been hung. Often used as dog food.

flesher: A sharp-edged flesh and hair scraper made from the leg bone (below the knee) of an animal, often the moose. Small fleshers are made from the bones of smaller animals.

flood plain: The highest level at which water will rise when rivers or lakes are flooded beyond normal levels.

freeboard: The amount of space between water and the upper edge (gunwale) of the side of a canoe or boat.

freeze-up: The time of year when rivers and lakes freeze over; the onset of the winter season.

fungus: A parasitic growth on trees, shrubs, and soil, including moulds, rust, mildew, smut, mushrooms, and bacteria.

green log: A newly fallen or harvested live tree, still moist with resin and water.

grouse: An upland bird; year-round resident of the boreal forest.

gullet: Throat or esophagus of a grouse.

gum: The sap of trees.

gunnel (gunwale): The upper edge of the side of a boat or canoe.

habitat: Natural environment of an animal or plant.

heel-dog (heeler): The dog which is hitched closest to the toboggan in a team of dogs hitched single file or tandem. Usually the largest and strongest dog in the team.

hew: To chop or cut and shape, with an axe or draw knife, to shape a log for building construction.

hitch: A number of dogs hitched to a toboggan (also known as a carryall or sled) in single file, tandem, or fanned out.

home base: The main residence of a trapper family.

Indian: A person registered or entitled to be registered under the Indian Act of Canada.

Indian hardwood: The larch (tamarack) tree, commonly used to construct snowshoe frames, and toboggan or sled runners; hard wood.

Indigenous: see Native.

jigger: An instrument used to feed a rope from a hole in the ice to another hole in the ice (on a river or lake). Once the rope is fed through from one hole to another, it is attached to a fish net and the net is pulled under the ice where it is set to catch fish. A jigger is two metres (six-and-one-half feet) long and a quarter of a metre (nine inches) wide, and is affixed with a hoop and rope to propel it under the ice.

kinnickinnick: A type of tobacco, given as an offering or used in spiritual rituals. Often the dried leaf of a bearberry plant or the bark of a red willow.

lapstick: A boat construction style. The bow and stern of a Chipewyan skiff may have side boards and top boards overlapping the bottom boards.

lead-dog: The dog at the head of a dog-team hitch; fast, sensitive to the moves of the team; alert to the commands of the dog musher; a highly trained member of the dog-team.

lichen: A plant organism, many-coloured, that grows on rocks and tree trunks. It is a food supply for some mammals and is often used to decorate traditional arts and crafts.

lick: (salt lick, animal lick) A natural outcrop of minerals (salt in particular) consumed by animals as a nutritional supplement; area in which one is located.

line cabin: A temporary residence used by a trapper, located on a trapline and usually within one working-day's travel from home base or another line cabin.

lobstick: A landmark used by a traveler; often consisting of a tall coniferous tree with only the topmost branches, leaves, and cones remaining; easily seen from land trails and water routes.

log built. Home or cabin built with logs.

long-hair: A designation given to fur-bearing mammals with a coat of long hair.

mainland: The main part of land, excluding islands.

Métis: People of mixed European and Aboriginal ancestry; unique to the cultural map of Canada in that they emerged only after the arrival of the European and the subsequent intermarriage of English or French Canadian men and First Nations women. Children born of these marriages were called "Métis", which is a French term for "mixed blood". The Métis history and culture draws on diverse ancestral origins, including Scottish, Irish, French, Ojibway, and Cree.

midwife: A person (typically a woman) who assists another woman in childbirth.

moccasin: Ankle-high footwear fashioned out of tanned hide for soles and out of hide or other fabric for ankle support.

moose-call: A cone-shaped megaphone made of birchbark, used by a hunter to imitate moose communication, usually imitating the mating messages of both male and female.

moss: As in bog, swamp, peat, peat moss: a clump of plants having a small, leafy, often tufted stem.

mukluk: Knee-high footwear fashioned out of tanned hide for soles and out of hide, fur, or other fabric for the section covering the ankle up to the knee.

muskeg: A marshy deposit of partly decayed vegetable matter, characteristic of northern regions.

Native: Belonging to a particular place by birth; belonging to or associated with one by birth. A reference to persons of Canadian Aboriginal ancestry, including people who are defined as Indian, Inuit, and Métis. Synonyms: Indigenous, Aboriginal.

Native Person: A member of a People who belong to or are descended from the original inhabitants of a region; in Canada, the term includes First Nations, Inuit, and Métis persons.

ochre: Native earth; hydrated peroxide of iron; coloured and used to decorate artwork.

off-season: A reference to times other than the trapping and hunting season; the post-breakup and pre-breakup times.

outboard: A motor which drives a propeller that pushes a boat over the surface of a lake or river, and which is attached to the outside of the stern of a boat.

outside: Somewhere much farther south of a northern residence.

overland: A travel route on land, as distinguished from travel across a water route.

pelt: Animal hide with fur attached.

pemmican: A mixture of dried lean meat (pounded into a fine powder) and rendered fat, along with the addition of berries for flavouring. Pemmican was high in protein and energy and was a staple of many Aboriginal and early fur-traders' diets as it could be stored for extended periods of time.

pitch: A naturally pliable compound (often ochre or tar), which seals cracks in wood, especially wood-built watercraft.

pole: A tree cut and trimmed and used as a tent pole, a pole of fencing or building enclosures; a teepee pole.

portage: An overland route across which boats, canoes, and provisions are carried between two bodies of water where passage may be difficult.

portaging: Refers to the act of carrying a boat or canoe and supplies over land to avoid obstacles or areas of rough passage in the water. During the fur trade era until the beginning of the 20th century, Aboriginals, explorers, fur traders, and voyageurs all traveled via water routes across North America. When there was a land break between two different water systems, these travelers would have to "portage" or carry their cargo and boat or canoe by foot across land to the next waterway. On a long portage voyageurs would often use packhorses to carry heavier cargo. It often took several trips to unload and carry the vessel and its content from one waterway to another. Some areas became known portage routes and gave rise to permanent settlements.

poultice: A compress applied to a flesh wound; a mixture of balsa sap and spruce needles boiled to reduce moisture and applied to a wound.

predator: An animal which seeks out, kills, and eats other animals. Humans are considered predators of animals.

prime: When used to talk about animal fur or pelts, refers to the time of the year when the fur is at its best condition. This usually occurs in winter, when the fur thickens to provide extra warmth for the animal.

ptarmigan: A bird belonging to the grouse family; unique to northern regions.

push-up: A muskrat den or habitat located underwater, the top of which is "pushed up" above the surface of the water or ice.

quill-work: Refers to the decorative work in which porcupine quills are dyed and sewn on to traditional arts and crafts objects, most often hide fabrics and birchbark crafts.

rat canoe: A small and very light watercraft (about three metres or ten feet long); used in shallow water for hunting in muskrat habitat.

rawhide: Refers to the stiff, white hide that emerges once the hair and flesh have been scraped off an animal hide that is hung and washed to dry but does not undergo the tanning process. It may be used in a variety of ways, including as a material for making drums and rattles. Once it has been soaked in resin, rawhide also makes excellent rope or binding and is especially durable when used as webbing for snowshoes.

reefer: A refrigerator or walk-in cooler designated for use by the entire community for the storage of food (mainly big game and fish). It is typically found in northern communities.

Reservation: (Reserve, Res) Parcels of land throughout Canada that were set aside and held in trust for the First Nations people of Canada after Confederation. Established in a series of Numbered Treaties and held in trust for the First Nations people by the government through the Department of Indian Affairs, these parcels of land were integrally connected to official "Indian" status and rights.

resin: A vegetable substance secreted by a tree, also known as tree gum or sap, that appears to sweat or ooze from the bark of the tree. It may be used as an adhesive or varnish.

ridgepole: The log that spans the upper ridge or peak of the roof of a log home, giving support to the roof.

ruff: Refers to the trim, usually made of strips of fur, that may be sewn to the hood of a parka to protect against severe weather. It may also be attached to the cuffs and rims of the parka for added decoration and weather protection.

rumen: Refers to the first stomach of the four-stomach digestive system of a number of animals including cows, moose, deer, and caribou, who must digest their food in two steps. Food is chewed and swallowed only to be regurgitated in a semi-digested form called cud, which is chewed and digested again. Rumen is a source of human food.

run-off: Accumulation of rainwater or snowmelt that runs over ground into lakes, streams, and sloughs.

rut (rut season): A season of the year; the mating season of moose, deer, caribou, or sheep. Hunting is made easier during the rut season, as the hunter can imitate animal mating calls and lure animals closer.

scabbard: A protective covering for a rifle, carried over the shoulder; usually made from tanned moosehide.

service community: A settlement, village, or town where food, clothing, and supplies are sold, traded or purchased and where social services are supplied.

set: A place where traps and snares are placed to catch animals.

shallow draft: A reference to a boat constructed to travel in shallow water, for example, a flat-bottomed skiff.

sheath: A protective covering for a knife, carried on the waist, made from tanned hide.

short-hair: A designation given small fur-bearing mammals with a shallow or short coat of fur.

sinew: A tendon; a fibrous cord connecting the muscle and bone of the neck of a moose, deer, caribou, and other members of the deer family. Sinew can be used in a number of ways, most often as a durable string or thread.

skiff (Chipewyan skiff): A flat-bottomed boat used for navigation across rivers or shallow waters; especially used for travel across fair-weather lakes.

skinning: The process of removing the skin (hide and fur) of an animal from the flesh; preparing an animal carcass by removing the hide to expose the meat for preparation.

sled (carryall): A toboggan about four metres (thirteen feet) long and half a metre (one-and-one-half feet) wide, fitted with a fabric (moosehide) sidewall cover; used to carry people and supplies; pulled by dogs, snowmobiles, or all-terrain wheeled vehicles.

sled dog: A work dog that pulls a toboggan.

smoke cure: The process of curing fish and meat by smoking it over a fire.

smoked: Meat or fish that is prepared by smoke-curing.

snare: An assembled system of roots, flexible branches, sinew, hide, rope, or wire that has been fashioned and set to catch mammals of all sizes (particularly fur-bearing animals).

snowshoe: A form of footwear one to two metres (three to seven feet long) with a prominent curve at the front, devised to allow for travel over soft, deep snow by distributing the weight of the traveller across a greater surface, thus preventing the traveller's foot from sinking into the snow.

sound ice: Lake or river ice that has frozen thick enough to travel over.

sounding ice: The process of determining the thickness of ice during the first stages of freezing by hitting the surface of the ice with a blunt instrument (usually the head of an axe) and being able to determine by the sound emitted whether or not the ice is thick enough to travel over.

spring camp: A place where a temporary camp is set up for the purpose of fishing or making dried meat, and for hunting for muskrat for fur.

stage: A platform comprised of poles; used to store fish, meat, and other supplies out of reach of carnivorous mammals.

stake: A stick or pole placed securely within the ground to which dogs can be tied or boats anchored to shore.

stick-built: Refers to homes or cabins that have been built from sawed or hewn timber, such as lumber.

stick of fish (fish stick): Dog food consisting of several (eight to ten) whole fish, weighing around ten kilograms (twenty-two pounds) in total, strung on to a sharp stick that has been pierced through the tail of each fish. Often, sticks totalling hundreds of fish are hung in the sun to dry.

Sweat (Sweat Lodge Ceremony): A traditional sacred Ceremony performed within a Sweat Lodge that involves the act of contemplating one's spiritual and physical well-being. Inside, a sacred fire heats special stones, waking the spirits living inside them. The stones are placed into a shallow pit at the centre of the lodge, often called the bellybutton of Mother Earth. The person residing over the ceremony then pours water over the stones, sending messages upwards to the Creator along with the rising steam. The steam cleanses the body of toxins, and heals the damage done to the soul. The ceremony may be presided over by an Elder, who receives and deciphers sacred messages.

Sweat Lodge: The Sweat Lodge is the place of healing and refuge in which the traditional Sweat Lodge Ceremony takes place. It is constructed out of willow branches which have been bent into the shape of a dome, and covered with blankets or animal hide to keep out light. Inside, a sacred fire heats special stones, waking the spirits living inside them.

tallow: Rendered animal fat fed to working sled dogs to supply them with energy. It may also be used as an energy supplement and cooking fat for humans.

tanning: The process of converting rawhide into a soft leather fabric that is used for a number of purposes, most specifically to make clothing.

Tea Dance Ceremony: A dance involving any number of people who dance side by side in a circle to the rhythm of drums; a social occasion.

Teepee (also known as Tipi): A housing structure used by Aboriginal Peoples, consisting of a conical frame of wooden poles covered with hide or commercial fabric. The teepee was very easy to transport from place to place, as its wooden base and canvas cover was simple to construct and deconstruct. It could be heated in the winter by a small central fire. The protruding smoke flaps could be shifted to catch the wind or be closed in rainy weather. Its tough hide walls were well anchored to the ground and therefore it remained snug and stable even during the work prairie storm. Special teepees could also be built as places in which to store and preserve food, i.e., a smoke-curing tent.

thong: A narrow strip of tanned hide, used as a string, rope, harness, handle, or strap.

traces: Leather straps; a portion of the harness by which dogs pull a toboggan.

trading post: A centrally located station or store at which groceries, trapline supplies, furs, artifacts, or cash could be traded or sold.

trail: A narrow, winding pathway leading to trapline sets, connection between trapline residences and service community; walkways of animals.

trapper: A person who sets traps, snares, and baits to lure an animal; a person who trades or markets the raw fur he or she catches; a person who makes a portion or all of his or her living off the resources of the land; a person who also hunts big game for food.

tree-line: The separation between forest land and barren land.

trim: See ruff.

underbrush: Shrub, grass, and plant growth that grows along the floor of a forest.

upstream: In the direction against the flow of the water in a stream.

upwind: Against the direction of the wind. Hunted game will seek a safe place to rest downwind from the suspected direction approach of predators.

watermark; waterline: A mark or stain visible on trees, shrubs, and lake or river banks that has been caused by water; an indicator of the seasonal level of lakes and rivers. To build a cabin above the waterline.

waterway: A traditional route travelled by hunters and trappers; a channel which is travelled by boat.

webbing: The material laced into the frame of a snowshoe. It consists of rawhide straps that have been strengthened and waterproofed with resin (the sap of trees).

whistler: a marmot; a mammal similar but larger than a ground squirrel. Its habitat is the mountain range. Its name is a result of the whistling sound of its call.

wolfdog: A hybrid resulting from the mating of a wild wolf with a domestic dog.

Glossary of bushland language ~ Cree

a-kis-kow (grouse): An upland bird; year-round resident of the boreal forest.

aku-pi-su-win (poultice): A compress applied to a flesh wound; a mixture of balsa sap and spruce needles boiled to reduce moisture and applied to a wound.

a-pa-suy (pole): A tree cut and trimmed and used as a tent pole; a pole of fencing or building enclosures; a teepee pole.

a-pe-to-wi-ko-si-san (Métis): People of mixed European and Aboriginal ancestry; unique to the cultural map of Canada in that they emerged only after the arrival of the European and the subsequent intermarriage of English or French Canadian men and First Nations women. Children born of these marriages were called "Métis", which is a French term for "mixed blood". The Métis history and culture draws on diverse ancestral origins, including Scottish, Irish, French, Ojibway, and Cree.

a-sa-was-si-kew (tanning): The process of converting rawhide into a soft leather fabric that is used for a number of purposes, most specifically as a material for clothing.

a-si-ne-wa-ko-nak (lichen): A plant organism, many-coloured, that grows on rocks and tree trunks. It is a food supply for some mammals and is often used to decorate traditional arts and crafts.

a-si-to-na-ya-sko (lapstick): A boat construction style. The bow and stern of a Chipewyan skiff may have side boards and top boards overlapping the bottom boards.

as-ki-ya (moss): As in bog, swamp, peat, peat moss: a clump of plants having a small, leafy, often tufted stem.

atim ota-pa-nask (sled, carryall): A toboggan about four metres (thirteen feet) long and half a metre (one-and-one-half feet) wide, fitted with a fabric (moosehide) sidewall cover; used to carry people and supplies across snow; pulled by dogs, snowmobiles, or all-terrain wheeled vehicles.

a-tis-ko-tas-kan (antler): The deciduous horn of a member of the deer family, i.e., moose, caribou, elk, or deer. Often used by Aboriginal peoples in the production of art, crafts, and tools.

at-tay (pelt): Animal hide with fur attached.

ay-wat-che-pi-me-miy (tallow): Rendered animal fat fed to working sled dogs to supply them with energy. It may also be used as an energy supplement and cooking fat for humans.

che-ma-nis (rat canoe): A small and very light watercraft (about three metres or ten feet long); used in shallow water for hunting in muskrat habitat.

e-wa-pe-ki-sit (prime): When used to talk about animal fur or pelts, refers to the time of the year when the fur is at its best condition. This usually occurs in winter, when the fur thickens to provide extra warmth for the animal.

E-yi-new, Na-he-yow (Indian): A person registered or entitled to be registered under the Indian Act of Canada.

Is-ka-ni-gan (Reservation, Reserve, Res): Parcels of land throughout Canada that were set aside and held in trust for the First Nations people of Canada after Confederation. Established in a series of Numbered Treaties and held in trust for the First Nations people by the government through the Department of Indian Affairs, these parcels of land were integrally connected to official "Indian" status and rights.

is-pa-to-wew (long-hair): A designation given to fur-bearing mammals with a coat of long hair.

Iye-niw (Native person): A member of a People who belong to or are descended from the original inhabitants of a region; in Canada, the term includes First Nations, Inuit, and Métis persons.

ka-sa-kew (predator): An animal which seeks out, kills, and eats other animals. Humans are considered predators of animals.

kas-ka-bas-wew (smoke cure): The process of curing fish and meat by smoking it over a fire.

kas-ke-wi-mes-ka-naw (portage): An overland route across which boats, canoes, and provisions are carried between two bodies of water where passage may be difficult.

kinnickinnick: A type of tobacco, given as an offering or used in spiritual rituals. Often consists of the dried leaf of a bearberry plant or the bark of a red willow.

kis-ta-gan (stake): A stick or pole placed securely within the ground to which dogs can be tied or boats anchored to shore.

kis-ti-ke-win (culture): Customary beliefs, values, and material traits of a racial or social group; the Aboriginal lifestyle.

ma-mik (downstream): In the direction of the flow of a river.

mas-ki-sin (moccasin): Ankle-high footwear fashioned out of tanned hide for soles and out of hide or other fabric for ankle support.

Ma-to-ti-san (Sweat Lodge): The Sweat Lodge is the place of healing and refuge in which the traditional Sweat Lodge Ceremony takes place. It is constructed out of willow branches which have been bent into the shape of a dome, and covered with blankets or animal hide to keep out light. Inside, a sacred fire heats special stones, waking the spirits living inside them.

Ma-to-ti-sow (Sweat Lodge Ceremony): A traditional sacred Ceremony performed within a Sweat Lodge that involves the act of contemplating one's spiritual and physical well-being. Inside, a sacred fire heats special stones, waking the spirits living inside them. The stones are placed into a shallow pit at the centre of the lodge, often called the bellybutton of Mother Earth. The person residing over the ceremony then pours water over the stones, sending messages upwards to the Creator along with the rising steam. The steam cleanses the body of toxins, and heals the damage done to the soul. The ceremony may be presided over by an Elder, who receives and deciphers sacred messages.

ma-ya-man (ochre): earth; hydrated peroxide of iron; coloured and used to decorate artwork.

me-chi-mi-ku-chi-kun (bait): Food, or an object that gives off the appearance, sound, or scent of food, used to lure an animal, bird, or fish into a trap.

me-ke-wap (camp): A residence, home, and property in the northern bushland.

mes-ka-naw (trail): A narrow, winding pathway leading to trapline sets; connection between trapline residences and service community; walkways of animals.

mik-kis-kaw (freeze-up): The time of year when rivers and lakes freeze over; the onset of the winter season.

mi-ki-wap (teepee, conical tent): A housing structure used by Aboriginal Peoples, consisting of a conical frame of wooden poles covered with hide or commercial fabric. The teepee was very easy to transport from place to place, as its wooden base and canvas cover was simple to construct and deconstruct.
It could be heated in the winter by a small central fire. The protruding smoke flaps could be shifted to catch the wind or be closed in rainy weather. Its tough hide walls were well anchored to the ground and therefore it remained snug and stable even during the work prairie storm. Special teepees could also be built as places in which to store and preserve food, i.e., a smoke-curing tent.

mi-mik-wan (scraper): A sharp-edged flesh and hair scraper made from the leg bone (below the knee) of an animal, often the moose. Small fleshers are made from the bones of smaller animals.

mis-tik-was-kos-kaw (boreal forest): A large area of wooded land; a dense growth of trees and underbrush, relating to northern and mountainous parts the northern hemisphere.

mi-wa-ti-gan, nu-ha-chi-kun (backpack): A container, usually of fabric construction, carried on a person's back and used to carry supplies.

Na-he-yow, E-yi-new (Indian): A person registered or entitled to be registered under the Indian Act of Canada.

na-mi-wan (downwind): In the direction towards which the wind is blowing; to be downwind from the location of a hunted animal.

na-na-kum (overland): A travel route on land, as distinguished from travel across a water route.

na-pa-ko-si (barged): Goods and supplies carried or transported across a river or lake by a barge either pushed or pulled by a power boat.

ne-me-hi-too-win (Tea Dance Ceremony): A dance involving any number of people who dance side by side in a circle to the rhythm of drums; a social occasion.

nes-ta-mo-tuk (bow): The front end of a canoe or boat.

ne-tu-se-ke-win (habitat): The natural environment of an animal or plant.

ni-pa-wi-ni-ku-mik (cabin): A small house located along a trapline used by trappers as a temporary residence or overnight shelter; usually built of logs and consisting of a single room.

ni-si-wa-na-ti-si-win (break-up): A time or season of the year, especially early spring; the movement and breaking of ice across lakes and rivers in the spring as caused by melting.

no-tchi-hit-tu-win (rut): A season of the year; the mating season of moose, deer, caribou, or sheep. Hunting is made easier during the rut season, as the hunter can imitate animal mating calls and lure animals closer.

nu-kwa-kun (snare): An assembled system of roots, flexible branches, sinew, hide, rope, or wire that has been fashioned and set to catch mammals of all sizes (particularly fur-bearing animals).

nu-na-to-we-hao (dry cure): A process of curing food, particularly meat and fish, in the open air over a trickle of smoke and heat from a wood fire.

nu-pa-ke-che-man (barge): A flat-bottomed boat capable of carrying freight across rivers and lakes, and pushed or pulled by a motor boat. Sizes range from a load capacity of two tons to six-hundred tons or more.

o-kes-ka-pa-se-ka-wisk-wew (midwife): A person (typically a woman) who assists another woman in childbirth; the one who cuts the umbilical cord.

oni-ka-pi-kew (portaging): Refers to the act of carrying a boat or canoe and supplies over land to avoid obstacles or areas of rough passage in the water. During the fur trade era until the beginning of the 20th century, Aboriginals, explorers, fur traders, and voyageurs all traveled via water routes across North America. When there was a land break between two different water systems, these travelers would have to "portage" or carry their cargo and boat or canoe by foot across land to the next waterway. On a long portage voyageurs would often use packhorses to carry heavier cargo. It often took several trips to unload and carry the vessel and its content from one waterway to another. Some areas became known portage routes and gave rise to permanent settlements.

o-ta-pa-ne-ya-piy (traces): Leather straps; a portion of the harness by which dogs pull a toboggan.

Ot-as-ki-niw (Aboriginal): Being the first of its kind in a region; a first person. In Canada, Section 35 of the Constitution Act of 1982 defined Aboriginal peoples to include First Nations, Inuit, and Métis peoples.

O-tit-to-wi-niw (Native): Belonging to a particular place by birth; belonging to or associated with one by birth. A reference to persons of Canadian Aboriginal ancestry, including people who are defined as Indian, Inuit, and Métis. Synonyms: Indigenous, Aboriginal.

o-wa-ne-hi-kew (trapper): A person who sets traps, snares, and baits to lure an animal; a person who trades or markets the raw fur he or she catches; a person who makes a portion or all of his or her living off the resources of the land; a person who also hunts big game for food.

pa-ko-tuk (deadwood): Trees, often a refuge for animals and birds; source of dry firewood.

pa-ku-new (skinning): The process of removing the skin (hide and fur) of an animal from the flesh; preparing an animal carcass by removing the hide to expose the meat for preparation.

pak-wat-chi-we-siw (short-hair): A designation given small fur-bearing mammals with a shallow or short coat of fur.

pak-we-si-gan (bannock): A heavy, flat, round bread made of flour, usually unleavened; a traditional recipe includes ground plant root and fish eggs.

pa-sit-che-pew (floodplain): The highest level at which water will rise when rivers or lakes are flooded beyond normal levels.

pe-che-ko-ma-nan (sheath): A protective covering for a knife, carried on the waist, made from tanned hide.

pe-kew (resin): A vegetable substance secreted by a tree, also known as tree gum or sap, that appears to sweat or ooze from the bark of the tree. It may be used as an adhesive or varnish.

pe-me-kan (pemmican): A mixture of dried lean meat (pounded into a fine powder) and rendered fat, along with the addition of berries for flavouring. Pemmican was high in protein and energy and was a staple of many Aboriginal and early fur-traders' diets as it could be stored for extended periods of time.

pes-we-pi-wey (down): The next-to-the-body layer of feathers of a goose or duck; used for stuffing pillows, quilts, and clothing, and as lining in bird nests. The eider duck (female) is a preferred source of down.

pi-kiw (pitch): A naturally pliable compound used to seal cracks in wood, especially wood-built watercraft, often ochre, tar, or tree resin.

pik-wa-tas-kiy (Barren Lands): Lands north of the boreal forest; a tract of land with inferior tree growth and little vegetation but rich in food for caribou and other mammals. It is a vast nesting habitat for many migrating birds.

pi-mik-wan (gunnel or gunwale): The upper edge of the side of a boat or canoe.

pi-mik-wa-na-tik (freeboard): The amount of space between water and the upper edge (gunwale) of the side of a canoe or boat.

pi-mi-pa-yit-chi-gan (outboard): A motor which drives a propeller that pushes a boat over the surface of a lake or river, and which is attached to the outside of the stern of a boat.

sa-ka-na-piy (thong): A narrow strip of tanned hide, used as a string, rope, harness, handle, or strap.

sa-ki-ku-paw (underbrush): Shrub, grass, and plant growth that grows along the floor of a forest.

se-ku-sa-ku-nuk (crackling): Also referred to as Indian popcorn, a sweet and crunchy snack made when the stomach cape of a moose is rendered to remove fat and then dried.

se-to-wu-hum (caulking compound): Material used to fill and seal the seams of boats and houses.

si-ta (brush): The low growth of shrubs and grass; often mixed with tree growth; a forest ground cover.

ta-ka-pit-chi-gan (hitch): A number of dogs hitched to a toboggan (also known as a carryall or sled) in single file, tandem, or fanned out.

tas-ki-pa-yiw (caulk/chink): The act of filling seams or joints of boats and log buildings to keep out air or water.

te-si-pi-che-gan (stage): A platform comprised of poles; used to store fish, meat, and other supplies out of reach of carnivorous mammals.

ti-ti-pa-we-yu-ku-hi-kun (quill-work): Refers to the decorative work in which porcupine quills are dyed and sewn on to traditional arts and crafts objects, most often hide fabrics and birchbark crafts.

uk-wa-hu-na-tak (deadhead, driftwood): A submerged log (tree) in a river or lake, one end exposed on the surface of the water, that may present a danger to navigation. The other end of the log is anchored in the lake or river bed.

us-ka-kin (rawhide, babiche): Refers to the stiff, white hide that emerges once the hair and flesh have been scraped off an animal hide that is hung and washed to dry but does not undergo the tanning process. It may be used in a variety of ways, including as a material for making drums and rattles. Once it has been soaked in resin, rawhide also makes excellent rope or binding and is especially durable when used as webbing for snowshoes.

us-ka-tick (green log): A newly fallen or harvested live tree, still moist with resin and water.

us-ke (mainland): The main part of land, excluding islands.

u-sam (snowshoe): A form of footwear one to two metres (three to seven feet long) with a prominent curve at the front, devised to allow for travel over soft, deep snow by distributing the weight of the traveller across a greater surface, thus preventing the traveller's foot from sinking into the snow.

us-tu-chi-ko-win (cache): A place for the storage of food and supplies; often located at strategic locations along the trapline and hunting route.

u-ta-wa-we-ku-mik (trading post): A centrally located station or store at which groceries, trapline supplies, furs, artifacts, or cash could be traded or sold.

u-tik-wu-ti-se (sinew): A tendon; a fibrous cord connecting the muscle and bone of the neck of a moose, deer, caribou, and other members of the deer family. Sinew can be used in a number of ways, most often as a durable string or thread.

u-tim (sled dog): A work dog that pulls a toboggan.

wa-ki-no-gan (Indian hardwood): The larch (tamarack) tree, commonly used to construct snowshoe frames, and toboggan or sled runners; hard wood.

was-ka-hi-gan-atik (log-built): Home or cabin built with logs.

was-ka-hi-ga-nis (line cabin): A temporary residence used by a trapper, located on a trapline and usually within one working-day's travel from home base or another line cabin.

was-ka-wa-ne-kwat-chi-gan (mukluk): Knee-high footwear fashioned out of tanned hide for soles and out of hide, fur, or other fabric for the section covering the ankle up to the knee.

was-kway (birchbark): The protective cover of a birch tree. Used traditionally to cover a canoe frame and used extensively in the production of crafts.

wa-pe-hyew (ptarmigan): A bird belonging to the grouse family; unique to northern regions.

wa-ti-kwan (boughs): The fine branches of a coniferous tree; often refers to the small branches of a spruce tree, as in spruce boughs.

wa-wi-ga-na-tik (ridgepole): The log that spans the upper ridge or peak of the roof of a log home, giving support to the roof.

we-yi-ne-hao (dressing): Preparing the carcass of a hunted animal, bird, or fish; removing hide (skin), some bones, and entrails.

wa-wi-ye-chi-wan (eddy): A place along a riverbank where the flowing water reverses its direction creating a circular flow of water; often still water bordered by a shore and a flowing stream; preferred place for travellers to rest or to place a permanent dock.

we-si-naw (castor): The large gland located under the belly skin of both male and female beavers, by which the scent of the beaver is carried and dispersed. It is a source of traditional medicine and a market commodity for the contemporary commercial perfume industry. In Cree, the word also refers to the scent from the castor of the beaver.

wi-ki, was-ki-hi-gan (home base): The main residence of a trapper family.

wu-ne-he-kao (set): A place where traps and snares are placed to catch animals.

ya-ye-ka-pe-si-ku-siw (candlestick ice): Lake or river ice which, in the spring, is near breakup condition. Not safe to travel over.

Resources of the land

Ash (from a wood fire)

Making Dye: Mixed with water, ash creates an iron-grey dye used to trace artistic patterns on hide fabric and bark.

Making Soap: Mixed with rendered fat or tallow (from moose or bear), ash is processed to make soap.

Anthill

A Trap Enclosure: Some ant colony populations are large. The home (hill) they build may be as large as two cubic meters (seventy-one cubic feet). Trappers will hollow out the hill and place bait inside to lure small fur bearing animals to a trap.

Ants

Bone Cleaning: Animal bone that needs to be cleaned of flesh is placed on an anthill. Dead flesh on bone is eaten by maggots, the larvae of the blowfly. The ants will go after the maggots, and remove them from the rotting flesh, prompting the blowfly to lay more eggs in the flesh. The ants will continue to remove maggots and the blowfly will continue to lay more eggs until the bone is cleaned of all the dead flesh on it.

Antler

Carvings: The antler of a deer, moose, caribou, or elk can be carved or shaped to transform it to an art or craft form. Images are carved into the antler or carved images are made from parts of the antler. Antler is softened by placing it in boiling water. It can then be shaped or carved with relative ease. As the antler cools, it hardens in the form it was shaped or carved.

Products: Antlers can be used as wall pegs, tent enclosure pegs, clothing hangers, and buttons.

Tools: Antlers are a source material for making a wide range of tools, including knife handles, buttons, and pegs.

Balsam

Poultice Compound: A mixture of balsam tree sap, bear fat, and the white liquid between the bark and trunk of the tamarack tree is applied to open wounds to draw out infection. A mixture of balsam sap and spruce needles, boiled to reduce moisture, serves as a poultice.

Bear

Claws and Teeth: Bear claws and teeth are fashioned as clothing accessories or as personal adornments like necklaces.

Fat: Bear fat is a clear (colourless) fat used as grease for frying and cooking. It is an excellent fat for deep-frying food, including bannock. Bear fat is also used in the production of soap.

Fur and Hide: A bear's hide is tanned and made into clothing, especially mitts, mukluks, and hats. The hide can also function as a floor or mattress covering, a blanket, or a toboggan covering for winter travel.

Gut: A bear's stomach can be cleaned and used as a container for the storage of fat or food.

Meat: Bear meat is edible and may be consumed boiled, dried, or roasted.

Tongue: The back of the bear's tongue, which is referred to as the worm, could be used to treat cancer.

Beaver

Castor: Mixed with rendered fat (bear or moose fat is preferred) shavings from a beaver's castor gland is a medicine when applied to human wounds or scabs.

Castor Gum: The wide base of a beaver's castor contains a gum-like substance which is chewed, often as medication for sore mouths.

Castorium: A beaver's castor gland produces castorium, an oily substance used in medicine and perfumery. For medicinal purposes, dry powdered castor is sprinkled on a small hot ember of wood or on heated stone or metal. The essence is breathed in to relieve a sore throat or nasal congestion. Castorium is the raw material for the production of perfume. Northern Canada is a source of raw castorium commercially traded to international perfume producers.

Foot Pin Cushion: After a beaver foot is dried, tanned hide is attached to its leg opening to form a cushion that is stuffed with hide fabric, hair, or wild cotton. This can be used as a pin cushion.

Bees

Hives: Beehives were saved and placed in the moss bag of a crying baby. It was said that the bees could sing the baby to sleep and ease the crying.

Berries

Beads: Berries may be preserved by drying, and are dried by exposure to sun and wind. Dried berries are used as beads to make crafts. A dried berry with a hole pierced through it is a bead to make necklaces and clothing applique.

Dye Colouring: Wild berries are a source of dye, used primarily to colour decorative fish scale, porcupine quill, and animal hair. There is a great variety of colour tints as a berry matures.

Food: Berries may be eaten raw or cooked. Dried berries may be mixed with meat and fat in the making of pemmican. Berries can also be rendered to make syrup, or prepared as jam. Most berries, boiled to produce juice, are a good source of syrup, jam, or fruit. Species and quantities vary by region. There are more than twenty berry species throughout the northern forest, with twelve species growing in relative abundance The favourites are cranberry (high bush, low bush, and bog), blueberry, chokecherry, strawberry, pin cherry, raspberry, dewberry, red currant, rosehip, and saskatoon. Some berries, the high-bush cranberry and the rosehip in particular, remain on the vine throughout the winter and can be picked and eaten frozen by birds, animals, or people. Buffalo berry (or its kin, soap berry) is crushed, and stirred continuously until it becomes foamy. It thickens and rises. When the foam rises to the top (of the container) sugar is added. It is stirred again until it hardens. When the foam hardens it turns into a light colour and is ready to be eaten. This is supposed to be good for diabetics.

Fruit Drink: Berries may be boiled to produce juice. This juice, in turn, can be mixed with water to make a refreshing drink.

Boughs

Floor and Mattress Covering: Spruce boughs, alone or in combination with dried moss, are an excellent ground cover on which bedding is placed. Spruce boughs also make good ground cover for a dirt floor in a temporary log cabin or a tent.

Mat: Spruce boughs may be used as a door mat and cover for wet muddy paths.

Shelter: Spruce boughs intertwined upright and staked in the ground or in a snowbank make a windbreak at an open camp.

Birch

Art and Crafts: A great variety of art forms can be created out of birchbark: baskets of many sizes, place mats, wall hangings, decorative tooth imprints, and many others.

Construction Material: Large strips of birchbark are pieced together and formed to make a canoe. Roof shingles on log homes are fashioned from large strips of birchbark as well.

Containers: Water buckets and bowls in a variety of shapes and sizes can be formed out of birchbark.

Source: The bark easiest to remove is from birch trees located close to a river or lake. Moisture through the roots and humid air absorbed by the bark makes these trees more pliable than trees exposed to dry wind or growing in dry ground.

Moose Call: This is a hunting horn used by a human to amplify and imitate the mating call of a moose. Birchbark is shaped as a cone. It is fifty to sixty centimetres (twenty inches to two feet) long. Spruce root or hide thong is stitched at the seam to secure the horn's shape.

Sap - Syrup: Spring is the time to tap a birch tree to drain the sap. Fourteen litres (three gallons) of sap is boiled down to produce four litres (almost one gallon) of syrup. Birch syrup may be flavoured and sweetened with dried berries. Red willow bark may be boiled with the sap to add a tint of brown to the syrup.

Birds

Wings - Duster: The wing of a bird is hung to dry in the breeze and heat of the sun. It is useful as a floor broom, a clothing duster, or a general purpose snow, dust, and small particles sweeper.

Bone

Fish-hook: Animal bone can be crafted into a barb of a fish-hook. A carved willow branch serves as a shaft. Sinew secures the shaft and the barb, and is looped to the shaft to connect to a line.

Flesher: A flesher is an instrument to scrape flesh and hair from a hide. It is normally made from the leg bone of a moose, but smaller fleshers from a deer are made to scrape fur pelts.

Knife: A butcher knife is made from the rib bone of a moose, caribou, or deer. This type of bone knife serves as a cutting and eating utensil, a flesher to clean hide, a scraping tool to remove scales from fish, and a blade to cut and form snow blocks.

Clay

Chinking Compound: Clay mixed with animal hair, grass, or moss makes a compound used to fill (chink) gaps between the logs forming the walls of a cabin.

Decomposing Wood

Curing Hides: Decomposing wood is commonly found in muskeg, and the smoke from its slow-burning embers is used in the traditional process of curing animal hides.

Duck, Goose, and Other Waterfowl

Bait: The feathered skin of a duck, a goose, or another waterfowl is used as bait for trapping fur-bearing animals.

Eggs: Duck, goose, or seagull eggs are used as ingredients in food preparation or eaten fried or hard-boiled.

Insulation: The feathers and down of ducks, geese, and other waterfowl make a good insulation for pillows, quilts, sleeping bags, and cold weather clothing.

Meat: Ducks, geese, and other waterfowls are a source of fresh meat during the late spring, summer, and early fall seasons.

Deer

Baby Cradle: Deerhide prepared to the white stage is often the material used to make a backpack to cradle an infant.

Fawn Hide Hand Bag: Because of its beautiful light brown background and white spots, the hide of a baby deer is highly desirable for the making of handbags.

Fish

Decorating: Fish scales are dyed with plant pigment and used to decorate clothing and artwork. Necklaces can also be made from dyed and stringed fish scales.

Dog Food: Whole fish, most often whitefish, are dried by suspending them on a stick suspended on a series of poles, or rack, exposed to the open air. A pointed willow branch is pierced through the tail of each fish. These "sticks" of fish, weighing nine kilograms (twenty pounds), are stored and fed to dogs as needed. Any species of fish may be fed whole, fresh, or frozen.

Eggs: Fish eggs are served fried, or they are added to a bannock (bread) mixture.

Fat: Fat from the stomach of a fish is rendered and used for cooking.

Fungus

Ground Fungus - Medical: The "powder puff" or "puff ball" fungus grows on the ground. It contains a dry brown powder which, when applied to a bleeding wound, will stop or reduce bleeding and ward off potential infection.

Tree Fungus - Fire Lighter: This fungus burns slowly and is an excellent medium for the containment of a smouldering fire. This smouldering fungus can be transported from one camp to another and be the ignition for the next campfire. A lit fungus is extinguished with water or by smothering it with soil.

Tree Fungus - Insect Repellent: Smoke from a smouldering fire in a tree fungus repels insects. It is a traditional form of a very much needed insect repellent and can be found and used for the same purpose today

Willow Fungus - Aromatic: The fungus that grows on willows has an refreshing aroma that serves as an air freshener. This fungus may be hung in a living enclosure or on a person.

Willow Fungus - Medical: This is somewhat like a sponge. When soaked with warm water or oil (fish oil or animal fat) it can be placed in the ear to relieve earache.

Grass

Broom: Long grass makes a useful broom or duster.

Chinking: Mixed with mud, grass is a holding compound to chink log houses. Grass mixed with clay creates a plaster for cabin fireplaces. Grass mixed with soil can be used as the roof cover of a house.

Fire Kindling: Dry grass is an excellent fire starter.

Trap Set: Long grass is used to cover traps. Animals are enticed by scents placed inside the grassy cover, opposite a one-sided opening. This forces the animal to cross the trap to get to the bait.

Grouse

Gullet - Baby Rattle: A grouse gullet, containing seeds, bark chips, and gravel is expanded by forcing air into it like a balloon. The opening is sealed with sinew or thong and the expanded gullet and its contents are left to dry hard. The dried gullet is used as an infant's rattle.

Tail - Fan: Grouse tail feathers have their own natural decorative markings, and can be used as a wall decoration or a hand fan.

Hair (Animal)

Bedding: Animal hair is used as stuffing for quilts and pillows.

Chinking: Animal hair mixed with clay is a chinking compound for log housing construction.

Tufting: Moose and caribou hair is dyed and used for tufting, a decoration on clothing and artifacts.

Hare and Rabbit

Blanket: As many as three rabbit pelts are cut into inch-wide strips, sewn in various lengths, and knit together to form an adult or crib-sized blanket. The same fabric is also knitted to make a sweater.

Clothing: The fur of a hare or rabbit is white only in the winter, and this is when it is most valuable. Hare fur is trim for all clothing, including moccasins and headgear. It adorns women's and children's clothing. Seldom is this fur used for men's clothing.

Droppings: If no other food source is available, the droppings of a male rabbit could be eaten. Droppings are eaten by rabbits and would be eaten by people near starvation.

Hide (Animal)

Backpack: The best material for a rugged backpack is the hide below the knee of a deer, moose, or caribou. The hair is short, and the skin is tough and waterproof. The hide of many legs, evenly sized as sheets of fabric, are pieced together with sinew and fashioned into a bag, the size to carry supplies on a person's back. The opening is rimmed with tanned moosehide. The carrying strap is a tanned or rawhide thong.

Blankets: Blankets are made from the hides of large animals, particularly bear and moose. A beaver pelt, with a backing of tanned hide and stuffed with dry moss, is a pillow.

Drum Cover: Drum cover fabric is prepared moose, caribou, or deerhide. The hide is secured with rawhide thongs over the face of a wood frame. The thickness of the hide and the tightness of the hide on the wood frame will determine the tone of the drum.

Thong, String, or Rope: Tanned or raw moose, deer, or caribou hide is used to tie packages and to make handles, moccasin laces, belts, or rope.

Kinnickinnick

Smoke, Offering: The ripened leaf of the bear-berry plant or the dried bark of the red willow shrub is finely ground into kinnickinnick, a tobacco to smoke. Kinnickinnick is a symbolic Offering used at formal occasions and at grave sites to honour the dead.

Larch

Hardwood: The larch tree, also known as tamarack, is the only cone-bearing tree that sheds its needles in the fall. Larch is also known to Aboriginal people as "Indian hardwood". This durable hardwood is used to build toboggan runners and snowshoes (see Tamarack).

Lime

De-wormer Medicine: Limestone, a land outcropping, disintegrates into powder when placed in high heat. Special ovens are built in banks of soil for this purpose. Lime powder, mixed with food, kills tapeworm, a parasite which invades the intestine of a dog.

Whitewash: Lime powder mixed with water is a whitewash used to paint log buildings.

Logs

Bear Trap: A bear trap is a three-wall log enclosure approximately two metres (six-and-one-half feet) high. Two logs are placed one above the other, midway between the side walls at the opening and the end of the enclosure. Two heavy logs are placed horizontally on the ground, one on top of the other. The top log is held three metres (almost ten feet) above the bottom log with a trip stick. A string is attached to the bottom of this trip stick and to bait. The bear enters the open end of the enclosure to retrieve the bait. As the bear pulls on the bait, the trip stick releases, causing the top log to fall on the bear, trapping it.

Construction: The forest yields logs for house building. Log construction is the mainstay for traditional dwellings.

Fish Trap: A fish trap is built with logs or stones either across a small stream, or protruding from the shore of a large stream. A trap may also be an abandoned beaver dam reconstructed by people. The trap is usually three metres (just under ten feet) long by two metres (six-and-one-half feet) wide and a metre (three-and-one-quarter feet) deep. Both sides, parallel to the stream flow, are built up with rocks or logs. There is an opening a few inches below the surface of the water, on the upstream and downstream ends of the trap. The fish move into the trap and swim below the top edge of the trap where they are momentarily obstructed. The trapped fish may be speared or scooped out of the water with a willow branch fork.

Food Cache: A food cache is a place for the storage of food and supplies. It is built at strategic locations along the trapline and hunting route, and especially at home base and at an overnight line cabin. It is built with logs big and strong enough to keep out scavengers as large as bears and wolverines and as small as mice, ravens, and whiskeyjacks.

Mint

Tea: Mint grass grows near small creeks and beaver dams. The leaves, fresh or dried, may be steeped in hot water to make a refreshing tea.

Lobstick

Signpost: Lobstick is a pine tree which may be ten metres (thirty-three feet) or more high with only the upper two or three metres (six-and-one-half to almost ten feet) of its branches remaining. It is a reference point, a trail marker along an overland trail or water travel route. It may indicate a stopover meeting place known to all travellers in the region.

Marmot

Blanket: Many marmot pelts are sewn together to form a blanket.

Storage Bag: The hide of a marmot is skinned out starting at its mouth. The feet and tail are removed at the knee joint so as not to leave a hole at these four points. The pelt, with the fur remaining on it, is turned flesh-side out and placed in the sun to dry and to be cleaned. It is turned back with the fur out. The only hole is the mouth. This bag is a storage container for rendered fat and other food (Virginia Rohatinsky, Grande Cache).

Maggots (Blowfly Larvae)

Bone Cleaning: A blowfly seeks out rotted animal or bird flesh to lay their eggs in. Maggots born of the eggs eat the dead flesh from animal bones. If a maggot infested bone is placed on an anthill, the ants will remove the maggots, which in turn will spur blowflies to lay more eggs in the remaining flesh. This process continues until the bones are cleaned of flesh. Cleaned bones may be used as utensils or tools. Aboriginal peoples used this process to clean animal parts when they wanted bone material (see Ants).

Moose

Backpack: Made from the strips of hide of the lower portion of the leg of moose, caribou, or deer. This hide is strong and with the short hair left on it is water repellent.

Bladder: The bladder is removed from the body of a moose, cleaned with water, and shaped by stuffing it with moss. The shaped bladder serves as a storage container for bear and moose fat.

Cape, Crackling, "Indian Popcorn": The cape from around the stomach of a moose is fried to remove the fat. The remaining fibre hung to dry is crisp (crackling) and edible.

Food: The chin, jaw, head, marrow, and ears of a moose are all eaten. The intestines of a moose are cut at the ends and waste, or rumen, is squeezed out to be cooked and consumed by people.

Mitts: The outside mitt is made from moose-hide. The liner is made with short hair, fur, or cloth. The fancy work is dyed hair, or dyed porcupine quill. A thong that extends from one mitt over the back of the neck to the next mitt permits the mitts to hang freely when working with bare hands.

Moccasin: Footwear common to many people is the plain, ankle-high moccasin, worn summer and winter. Moccasins are made from moosehide, and hair tufting, fish scales, porcupine quills, or dried berries are often sewn on for decoration. The style will often indicate whether the footwear is to be worn by a man or a woman.

Mukluks: This is footwear which covers the leg from the foot to below the knee. The thickest portion of tanned moosehide is preferred for the sole of footwear. Other hide or fur may be used for the upper portion. Thongs (strips of hide) are used to tighten the top around the leg and to secure the mukluk on the foot.

Rifle Carrying Case: Tanned moosehide can be formed to cover a rifle to protect it from rain and soil. An attached shoulder strap serves to free the hands while the rifle is carried on the back. Sinew thread sews the hide strips. Tanned hide rims the opening, and a tanned hide thong serves as the carrying strap.

Snow or Sun Blindness Relief: Around the womb or uterus of the moose there are three-centimetre nodules. They are removed from the moose and pressed to the eyes to relieve the effects of strain caused by the glare of snow and sun.

Moss

Bedding and Insulation: Moss is often used as log chinking and insulation and as stuffing for mattresses and pillows.

Sanitary Uses: Moss is a low tufted herbaceous plant which grows on damp soil and on the surface of stones and trees. It is commonly found in bog, peat-bog, or wet, spongy land. The top of the moss plant is discarded. The next layer, light brown and soft, is the best for diapers and sanitary use around the home.

Ochre

Building Product: Mixed with grass it is a chinking compound for log houses. It adds colour to the building.

Decoration: This is native earth consisting of hydrated peroxide of iron with clay. Its colour and its stiff and pliable consistency make it a popular decorative application used by artists.

Otter

Tail: An otter's tail, in the place where it is greasy, could be rubbed on the neck to ease a sore throat.

Pelican

Pouch: The pouch from the jaw of a pelican, when slightly modified, is a carrying pouch for people. Small items such as medicine, water, and artwork material (needles, thread, moose hair, fish scales porcupine quills are carried in this pouch.

Poplar

Black Poplar - Medicine: The liquid layer of sap under the bark of a black poplar tree is applied to an open wound, usually after it is refined by chewing.

Sap - Food: The poplar tree oozes a sap that has the flavour of rhubarb.

White Poplar - Food: The white material layered under the bark of white poplar can be eaten as it is scraped off. It is primarily an emergency food supply.

Porcupine

Meat: Classed as white meat, porcupine is close to the texture of domestic chicken.

Quill - Decoration: Dyed in many colours, porcupine quills are sewn or braided to decorate crafts and clothing.

Sinew

Thread: Sinew taken from the neck of a moose, deer, or caribou is made up of hundreds of fibres, each of which can be separated and used singularly or bunched to make whatever sized thread or string is needed.

Skunk

Hide or Scent Glands: These were placed on a tree near the home or on the house to symbolically ward off illnesses.

Medicine: Skunk oil from the skunk's scent glands is mixed with water, and the yellowish mixture is applied with a sponge or a cloth to the gums to relieve toothache or is rubbed on a person to soothe chest pain or relieve itchy skin. Skunk spray mixed with water can also be used to medicate a sore throat.

Spruce

Needles: Spruce needles mixed with balsam or spruce sap, when boiled to reduce water, makes a poultice to draw infection out of an open wound (see Boughs).

Roots: Sewing lace and bindings are made out of spruce roots. The raw root is pulled through a narrow opening in a branch to remove the outer cover of the core of the root. It is made pliable by boiling it in water. After the root has dried, grease is applied to it to help it retain its flexibility. Spruce root string is used to bind, sew, lace, or string together baskets, canoes, and artifacts.

Tamarack

Carryall Mainframe: Tamarack trees are the source of wood runners for a toboggan (carryall).

Tallow

Dog Food: Tallow, or rendered animal fat, is fed to sled dogs. It is a high energy food supplement, especially important on working days and long trips.

Tree

Bark - Dye or Colouring: Tamarack or red willow bark boiled in water produces dye.

Bark- Roof Shingles: Large strips of birch or spruce bark could be used as roof shingles.

Bark or Root - Fish Snare: A strip of green tree bark or small root, looped as a noose, is attached to the end of a hand-held stick. The fish, seen in a clear shallow stream, is caught as it moves through the noose.

Resin: Resin is a vegetable substance secreted by trees and can act as a natural preservative in wood canoe construction.

Wood - Baby Rattle: A common style of wooden baby rattle is circular, flat style with a handle. One end of a strip of wood is curled to form an enclosed circle while the other end of the strip remains straight, to be used as a handle. The wood circle is covered with tanned hide in which stones are enclosed. The seam is sewn shut with sinew or hide thongs.

Wood - Drying Rack for Fish and Meat: A rack is a series of horizontal poles suspended by other poles secured vertically in the ground. A rack may also be in the shape of an A-frame. Animal meat and fish are placed on these poles to be cured and flavoured by smoke from a smouldering fire below the rack and from the heat of the sun above it.

Wood - Paddles: The jack pine, spruce, or birch tree is a common source of wood for canoe paddles and boat oars. Jack pine wood is preferred because it has a natural abundance of resin. Resin reduces the rate of rot caused by exposure to moisture.

Wood - Snowshoes: The wood of various trees in the boreal forest can potentially be used in the making of snowshoes, though birch is the preferred wood for a snowshoe frame. Animal products are also used to make a snowshoe. Sinew or rawhide is latticed in the frame, while hide thongs hold the snowshoe to the foot. Snow, sheltered from the wind in dense bush, remains deep and relatively loose, and snowshoes help pack down snow on trails, and help keep a person from sinking deep. Snow in the Barren Lands is packed by wind and drifting and becomes hard enough to walk on. Snowshoe style may vary according to the nature of the snow and the culture of the people.

Willow

Branches - Sweat Lodge: Sweat Lodges are domed structures tall enough to sit in and large enough to hold six to eight people. Willow branches are used to make the framework of Sweat Lodges, and leaves or fabric provides a cover for the frame.

Index